D0313361

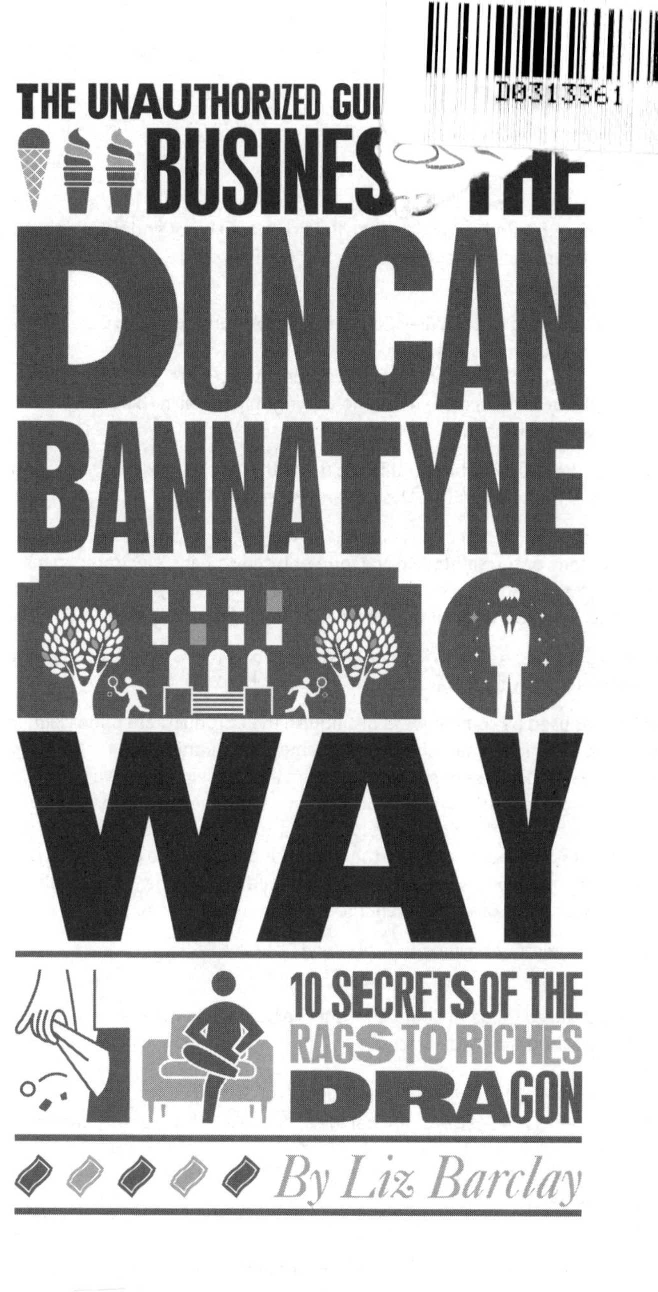

30131 05013708 9
LONDON BOROUGH OF BARNET

This edition first published 2010
© 2010 Liz Barclay

The Unauthorized Guide To Doing Business the Duncan Bannatyne Way is an unofficial, independent publication, and Capstone Publishing Ltd is not endorsed, sponsored, affiliated with or otherwise authorized by Duncan Bannatyne.

Registered office
Capstone Publishing Ltd. (A Wiley Company), The Atrium, Southern Gate, Chichester, West Sussex, PO19 8SQ, United Kingdom
For details of our global editorial offices, for customer services and for information about how to apply for permission to reuse the copyright material in this book please see our website at www.wiley.com.

The right of the author to be identified as the author of this work has been asserted in accordance with the Copyright, Designs and Patents Act 1988.

All rights reserved. No part of this publication may be reproduced, stored in a retrieval system, or transmitted, in any form or by any means, electronic, mechanical, photocopying, recording or otherwise, except as permitted by the UK Copyright, Designs and Patents Act 1988, without the prior permission of the publisher.

Wiley also publishes its books in a variety of electronic formats. Some content that appears in print may not be available in electronic books.

Designations used by companies to distinguish their products are often claimed as trademarks. All brand names and product names used in this book are trade names, service marks, trademarks or registered trademarks of their respective owners. The publisher is not associated with any product or vendor mentioned in this book. This publication is designed to provide accurate and authoritative information in regard to the subject matter covered. It is sold on the understanding that the publisher is not engaged in rendering professional services. If professional advice or other expert assistance is required, the services of a competent professional should be sought.

Library of Congress Cataloguing-in-Publication Data

Barclay, Liz.
The unauthorized guide to doing business the Duncan Bannatyne way : 10 secrets of the rags to riches dragon / by Liz Barclay.
p. cm.
Includes bibliographical references and index.
ISBN 978-1-907312-35-9 (pbk. : alk. paper) 1. Success in business. 2. Entrepreneurship. I. Title.
HF5386.B2298 2010
658.4'09--dc22

2010000251

A catalogue record for this book is available from the British Library.

Set in Myriad Pro by Sparks (www.sparkspublishing.com)
Printed in Great Britain by TJ International Ltd, Padstow, Cornwall

CONTENTS

ACKNOWLEDGMENTS

It's been a joy reading about Duncan Bannatyne's business operations. As one of the UK's best-known serial entrepreneurs, his story is fascinating and his approach to business is practical and inspiring.

I would like to thank my wonderful, tenacious, dedicated and insightful researcher Hannah Matthews, who has helped me so much with writing this book about the way Bannatyne does business. Without her I would have died of exhaustion. She has watched every episode of *Dragons' Den* and read every word ever written by Bannatyne and about him. Thank you!

I'd also like to thank Holly Bennion, Jenny Ng and the rest of the team at Capstone for giving me the opportunity to write this book and for their support and guidance. And my grateful thanks to my business partner Tony Fitzpatrick for taking care of all the other aspects of my working life while I've been otherwise occupied.

At the back of the book there's a list of all the articles and websites we've used in research, including Bannatyne's own books – his autobiography *Anyone Can Do It: My Story* and his other bestseller *Wake Up and Change Your World*, which is full of advice on how to run your business from the man himself. Both these books are excellent further reading, with more detail on his life story.

THE LIFE AND TIMES OF DUNCAN BANNATYNE

Duncan Bannatyne OBE, 167th in the *Sunday Times Rich List*, is one of the UK's most successful 'serial' entrepreneurs, with a portfolio of leisure businesses and a high-profile media career. There's the tough businessman who started in ice cream and built a portfolio of 61 health clubs, the hotels, the bars, the spas and the residential property development. There's the sharp, opinionated Duncan Bannatyne, who regularly gives would-be entrepreneurs a drubbing in the BBC series *Dragons' Den*. And there's the philanthropic nice guy who was awarded an OBE in the 2004 Queen's Birthday Honours for his services to charity.

WHO IS DUNCAN BANNATYNE?

He is the serial entrepreneur who claims to have simply done what anyone else could have done. He makes much of his lack of qualifications and business background. He prides himself on having built a business empire without having had an original idea. He claims to hate details and that he's not a good manager. He admits to being good with figures, is proud of the gut instinct he uses when recruiting staff and the quick thinking that allows him to spot a constant stream of business opportunities. He puts his success down to delegation and common sense. His winning streak is down to determination, taking opportunities as they arise and an ability to approach a problem in a new way.

Yet he's a man of contradictions. His books are full of classic, accepted business wisdom, while he claims to have taken little of that kind of advice. He wonders whether he was a 'born' entrepreneur, while reassuring his readers that anyone can do it. He sees himself as a maverick but, in the view of *Dragons' Den* presenter Evan Davis, can make fairly conservative investment decisions. He has an innate dislike of authority yet seems to delight in consorting with the political and business 'establishment'.

He eschewed the usual business network opportunities like the golf course and the Freemasons, yet he was very keen to build a public profile that would help him grab the attention of the policy-makers. He has disdain for 'usual practice' and delights in breaking the mould, but has been accused of being controlling. He claims to be good with people and yet doesn't want to manage them. He makes no apology for wanting to go on making more money and for being prudent with what he has made, yet he intends to give the vast majority of it away before he dies. He claims to have felt the presence of God on one of his charity missions, but isn't ready to turn to religion because – as he jokingly told a reporter on the *Darlington and Stockton Times* a week before he married a second time – 'I still suffer from greed, abhorrence [and] coveting of my neighbour's wife'.

He's also a man of inconsistencies. His views on a subject, and his own actions, can change as and when required – for the good of his business and perhaps sometimes his pride. Even when he's wrong, he's right. Even when he's made a mistake, he turns it to his advantage. This is a man unlikely to say 'sorry'. But then again, we don't expect him to … he's staked his brand and reputation on being right.

However, he can on occasion be almost too consistent to be entirely believable. When he's interviewed, the answers are often the same. His home life, school days, stint in the Navy, brush with prison life, the rags to riches story, are all recounted 'pat', practised and packaged for public consumption. It's all part of the brand.

While the man has become rich, his profile has given him kudos and his fame has endeared him to even more famous friends. It's hard to find a celebrity who doesn't attract admiration and loathing in almost equal measure. Bannatyne has attracted the wrath of some of his siblings, the *Daily Mirror* and Facebook's 'I hate Duncan Bannatyne' group, but in the main he seems to have achieved the status of a slightly grumpy uncle. He's rather politically incorrect: you know the kind of thing he'll say, but you'll roll your eyes heavenward and let him off with it.

Duncan Bannatyne enjoys business and may well also enjoy the money that comes from business success. But he is an enigma: despite it being what he does best, he says it's not about the money. He says what drives him is being able to give people what they need and give them the best. So how did Duncan Bannatyne get from what he describes as a 'two up, two down' in Clydebank near Glasgow via the Navy to multi, multi-millionaire? Why did someone who has so many of the natural attributes of an entrepreneur take so long to get going?

IN THE BEGINNING ...

Duncan Bannatyne was born in February 1949. His father, Bill, had served with the Argyll and Sutherland Highlanders and had been a prisoner of war, while mum Jean packed shells with cordite at a munitions factory in Glasgow. They married in 1946 and Duncan was the second of a family that eventually grew to seven children. He claims to have inherited his determination from his dad, but always wanted life to be more exciting than it was.

The way Bannatyne remembers it, as a child, his parents couldn't always afford ice cream when the van came round the local streets.

He was determined that one day he'd be the one to buy ice creams for all his family. But the crunch came when he asked his dad for a bike, only to be told the family was too poor. So he made up his mind to buy his own.

A couple of boys at school had paper rounds, so Bannatyne asked for a job at the local newsagent but got turned away. But he wouldn't give in and cold-called everyone in his vicinity, asking if they'd like a paper delivered. Armed with a list of 100 would-be customers, he went back to the newsagent and got the job. Even if he didn't recognize it himself – 'When I was a kid no one had ever heard of the word "entrepreneur" in Clydebank.'[1] – the entrepreneur in him had been unleashed.

Eventually his enterprise paid off and he bought a second-hand bike on HP. A few months later he had enough money to buy the whole family ice cream from the van!

FAMILY FRACAS

Bannatyne's family dispute his version of their childhood. When his account of family poverty came to light in his autobiography *Anyone Can Do It: My Story*, it caused a family rift that hasn't been resolved. In January 2009 his brother Sandy told the *Daily Mirror* that he hasn't spoken to Duncan since, that 'I can honestly say I can't stand the man' and that the book contains inaccuracies and upset the family. His brothers say they always had enough clothes, shoes and food in their three-bedroom family home; Bannatyne counters this by saying that he didn't say they weren't well fed and clothed, and maintains that his parents worked hard for their family.

Some family members might have been upset at his remarks about their lack of drive and ambition (which Bannatyne has said in interviews wasn't a criticism, but just meant to point out that he was different), but it seems to be their perception of him as not being generous with the family that's at the bottom of the row. Sandy famously signed up to the 'I hate Duncan Bannatyne' Facebook group and the *Daily Mirror* enjoys reigniting the fury at every opportunity.

Whatever the details of his early family life, Bannatyne left school at 15 with no qualifications and a reputation for being a bit of a troublemaker. Already restless, he seems to have been easily bored with an entrepreneurial mind that was looking for something else to get involved in – the kind of mind he shares with so many other successful business people.

All he knew was that he didn't want to end up working in the sewing machine factory in Clydebank like his father and that he wanted travel and adventure – so he joined the Royal Navy. Because he wasn't yet 16 he needed his parents' permission, but his mother refused. He applied emotional blackmail, threatening to run away to London and live as a tramp and a junkie, so eventually she gave in. Six weeks' work experience with the local cabinetmaker did nothing to change his mind.

ALL AT SEA

Duncan Bannatyne arrived at the boys' naval training base near Ipswich at the age of 15. It had a reputation for harsh training methods that turned out professional sailors. He signed up to spend the next 12 years in the engine room as a stoker.

His first commission was on HMS *Eagle* in British waters, but by 17 he was well travelled. However, he already knew the Navy wasn't for him and was wondering how much trouble he'd have to get himself into to get chucked out. Rules and regulations weren't to Bannatyne's liking and nor were commissioned officers with their university educations – according to his autobiography and various other interviews he's given, he didn't see eye to eye with his commanding officer.

Eventually, matters came to a head in Lossiemouth when Bannatyne lifted the officer into the air and hoisted him over the rail. Bannatyne says in some interviews that he was dared to do it. The officer found himself dangling 20 feet above the dark, icy waters of the North Sea. Luckily he was restored to the deck unharmed, but Bannatyne had done enough to get himself a court martial. He was sentenced to nine months in Colchester Barracks and a dishonourable discharge. His mother found out on the local evening news.

DRIFTING

After his discharge the 19-year-old, unemployed Bannatyne went back to Clydebank and his parents, and signed up to a training course to become an agricultural vehicle welder and fitter. Not exactly the stuff of an entrepreneur's dreams, but between that and bar work he managed to afford driving lessons, bought a car and over the next few years drifted around the UK fixing tractors, pouring drinks, driving taxis and mending cars. Almost without realizing it, he started his first business. He'd buy a car at auction, repair it and use it as a taxi. When he could afford another car, he got a friend to drive it … and then another.

However, the untimely passing of his sister temporarily led Bannatyne down a dark road. By his own account, he became belligerent after her death and lost his licence for drink driving. It took another period of travelling the UK taking work as a welder and fitter, a few arrests and a three-day stay in Glasgow's overcrowded and dangerous Barlinnie Prison to convince him the time had come to do something more positive. He regularly makes the point in interviews that he was teetering on the edge of a criminal lifestyle and it could have gone either way.

Bannatyne finally washed up in the Channel Islands, where he found bar work, women, surfing and life-long friendships, had fun, and learned about running a business.

THE END OF THE BEGINNING

One of the easiest ways to make money in Jersey was to sell ice cream, so he rented a van, paid extra for an exclusive pitch and bought some stock. If it was a festival day, Bannatyne could earn enough to take the rest of the month off. What he probably discounted then was what he was learning about running a business. Ice cream was to play quite a big part in eventually launching Bannatyne on the road to riches.

Before he realized it he was approaching 30, living with his girlfriend Gail (who later became his first wife) and felt in danger of becoming the 'oldest swinger in town'.[2] One Sunday morning he read an article about Alan Sugar and how he'd set up Amstrad on a shoestring ten years earlier and became a millionaire. Bannatyne was impressed and inspired by Sugar's achievements from humble beginnings.

So Gail and Duncan left Jersey in 1978 for Stockton-on-Tees, to see Gail's sister. They stayed and worked nightshifts at Spark's Bakery. Bannatyne bought cars at auction to do up and sell on. They saved every penny. They worked through the bread strike of 1978, crossing the picket line despite threats and shouts of 'scabs', and after about a year put down a deposit on a three-bedroom semi-detached house. They were moving up in the world; two weeks later, Bannatyne saw his business opportunity and took it.

ON THE ROAD TO RICHES

A Vauxhall ice cream van cost Bannatyne £450 at auction. It was too low for him to stand up in with his shoes on. He looked up 'Ice cream supplier' in the *Yellow Pages*, found the best deal and bought enough stock for a weekend. Once he'd worked out what sold well he stocked the van with cigarettes, milk, sweets and soft drinks as well as the ice cream. 'Duncan's Super Ices' was up and running.

Bannatyne showed entrepreneurial flair – the kind of thing that can't be taught. He seems to have known instinctively that Duncan's Super Ices needed to stand out from the crowd. Others were moving into selling soft ice cream that was quick to serve but Bannatyne wanted to stick with the more traditional hard stuff, so he bought a special ice cream scoop from the USA. It allowed him to serve his hard ice cream as quickly as others served soft ice cream.

His entrepreneurial flair made life difficult for the competition and if they struggled and wanted out of the business, he then bought their vans and hired friends on commission as drivers. Bannatyne understood the value of being the only ice cream seller allowed on a particular pitch. So when a local authority concession that guaranteed he'd be the only ice cream vendor in one of the local parks was advertised for sale, he bought it, even though it cost him £2000. It was a brilliant business move that other sellers didn't seem to see the value of.

The business expanded from one van to a small fleet with an annual turnover of around £300,000, but Duncan Bannatyne still wanted more.

AND MORE ... AND MORE

The money from the ice cream business was enough to buy and do up terraced houses to let out. In the early 1980s the government paid £46 a week directly to landlords who rented homes to unemployed people. Duncan converted his houses to bedsits and happily took £46 a week for each.

Occasionally he was asked to rent a place out to an elderly person, which set him thinking about the need for residential care. Then the government played into his hands again and promised £140 a week for every elderly person who needed looking after. He and a business partner bought a six-storey hotel in Scarborough with planning permission. He turned it into a residential home for the elderly. It was a brief foray into business partnership. The next phase of the Bannatyne empire, however, was launched alone.

AND THE REST IS HISTORY

The next step was into nursing homes with added value – places he'd be happy for his mum to live in. Quality Care Homes made Bannatyne relatively rich when the company was floated on the stock market in 1992. He sold his remaining shares in 1997 but his next venture had already launched. Just Learning was a chain of children's nurseries or day care centres. The first one opened in 1996 and the business sold for £22 million in 2000. Bannatyne Fitness was added to the portfolio in 1997 and has grown into the largest independent health club operator in the UK.

Add to that a few hotels and spas, residential property, and a very high profile media career, you get Duncan Bannatyne OBE, serial entrepreneur and seriously rich man. Bannatyne has also become a Business Angel, investing in other people's businesses and giving them a helping hand with his expertise. He's very involved in charity work, particularly in Romania and Malawi, and is determined to make his wealth count. At the minute that wealth is estimated to be around £320 million and counting. His children will benefit from small trust funds – which famously they won't get their hands on unless they stick to the rules dad has set down about smoking and drink driving. The rest (about 95% of his fortune) will go to charity.

THAT'S BANNATYNE, NOT BALLANTYNE!

After years of mistakenly being called 'Ballantyne', the Bannatyne name is now instantly recognizable. These days his businesses have 'Bannatyne' above the door and he sometimes jokes that it's not just because he wants to teach the world to spell! Bannatyne has become a household name through TV programmes such as *Dragons' Den*, *Fortune* and *Mind of a Millionaire*, and books including his autobiography *Anyone Can Do It*. The name is the brand.

BEEN THERE, DONE THAT

A brief history of Duncan Bannatyne' s career:

- **1949–64:** Born in Clydebank, Scotland. Left school with no qualifications and joined the Royal Navy.
- **1968:** Dishonourably discharged from the Navy onto the dole.
- **1972–4:** Oldest sister died. Lost his driving licence and business, and spent three days in Glasgow's notorious Barlinnie Prison.
- **1974–8:** Enjoyed a carefree life in Jersey with future wife Gail. Learned the ice cream trade and moved to Stockton-on-Tees.
- **1979–84:** Married Gail and grew his ice cream business to a turnover of £300,000 a year.
- **1984–6:** Bought and did up terraced houses for rent to unemployed people, and moved from there into the care business. Each room in his nursing homes had its own toilet facilities – unheard of in care homes until then.
- **1986–91:** Quality Care Homes expanded quickly.

- **1992:** Floated Quality Care Homes on the Stock Exchange. The company was valued between £17–20 million; £4 million was paid into the company bank account and £500,000 into Bannatyne's personal account. He owned 72.8% of the company.
- **1992–5:** Began to get involved in charity, both personally and as a company. Visited Romania and resolved to make a lifelong commitment to the children in the orphanages there.
- **1993–5:** Injured his leg in a skiing accident and saw the potential of the health business as he recuperated in a gym. Divorced Gail. Sold shares in Quality Care Homes to give her almost half his wealth. He still owned 50.8% of the company.
- **1995–6:** Launched Just Learning.
- **1996–2003:** Used his expertise to turn around other businesses, including a radio station and a sheltered housing firm. Lost £1,040,000 in a failed ladies-only gym business. Went into the hotel business and began building the first Bannatyne Health Club.
- **1997:** Got involved with Unicef. Sold Quality Care Homes for £46 million, of which he received £26 million. Opened the first Bannatyne Health Club.
- **1997–2007:** Bannatyne Fitness expanded rapidly, becoming the UK's largest independent fitness chain. Moved into housing. Was offered £120 million for Bannatyne Fitness, but rejected it. Sold Just Learning for £22 million. Funded a children's hospice in Romania and Casa Bannatyne opened there.
- **2002–5:** Tried his hand at acting. Was awarded an OBE for services to business and charity.

- **2005:** First appeared on *Dragons' Den*. Wealth quoted on the show as £130 million. Other TV shows followed. Opened a casino in Newcastle upon Tyne that closed in 2006.
- **2006:** Married his long-term partner Joanne. Published his autobiography, *Anyone Can Do It*. Awarded an honorary Doctorate of Science from the University of Glasgow.
- **2007:** Bannatyne Fitness bought the Living Well chain of gyms from Hilton Hotels for £92 million. The *Sunday Times Rich List* estimated his wealth at £200 million.
- **2008:** Founded the Bannatyne Charitable Trust; opened the £12 million Bannatyne Spa Hotel in Hastings and revamped his spa chain. Wealth now estimated at £310 million on the *Rich List*.
- **2009:** Awarded a Doctorate of Business Administration (DBA) from the University of Teesside. Estimated wealth £320 million. Appeared in the seventh series of *Dragons' Den*.

COMING IN FOR CRITICISM

Bannatyne often repeats that he's not just working for the money – it's about doing the best possible job and giving more to his customers. He has built his business on that ethos. Of course people who are in the public eye and do well financially come in for criticism, and Duncan Bannatyne hasn't escaped.

It's not just his family who are critical: there are the stories of the witch hunt to discover which member of staff ate two boiled eggs left over from lunch; his second wife's admission that while employed by him she sometimes had to mop up the tears of some of his hard-pressed employees who felt he was aggressive; and a row over selling what were supposed to be complementary cereal bars in his health centres, although he was emphatic he had done nothing wrong. But Bannatyne makes no apology for making money and wanting to make more money.

He's also been berated for penny pinching, although he sees this as cautious and prudent (perhaps that aptly Scottish word 'canny' is more appropriate); for being ruthless, for which he substitutes bloody-minded and determined; and for being arrogant – which even he has admitted some people do find him to be. Could business people be so successful if they weren't tough?

But any criticism he's attracted over the years seems to have done him no harm either personally or business-wise; many of his employees have been with him for a long time and for all his detractors his supporters seem to be legion.

WORK-LIFE BALANCE

There were times when work took over his life and the desire to build the business drove him on. His first rule of business is that to succeed you have to work as hard as it takes. These days he can delegate to his teams, write books and make TV programmes, but when he was setting up his new ventures he worked anything up to 18-hour days for months at a stretch. He says you have to do what it takes and possibly do the work of several people until the thing is up and running.

But he also argues that ultimately the business is there to give you the lifestyle you want rather than being all-consuming. The ice cream business allowed him to spend time with his young daughters because he worked afternoons and weekends. Once they were at school the hours were less convenient – he was going to work as they came home. So he delegated Saturdays to an employee and looked for a more nine-to-five business. It's a pattern he tried to follow as his businesses grew and delegation is the key.

So from rags-to-riches, from trouble making schoolboy to OBE, from unemployment benefit claimant to multi-millionaire, the following chapters aim to explain the ten secrets that Duncan Bannatyne has applied to business.

1
ANYONE CAN DO IT

'I've done it and I'm thick. For Christ's sake, Peter Jones [fellow *Dragons' Den* judge] is thicker than me and he's done it.'[1]

– Duncan Bannatyne

SO CAN ANYONE DO IT?

If you read the biographies of entrepreneurs you'll find some who came from business families, went through business schools, started with a helping hand from dad or took over the flourishing family operation. And you'll find those who did it another way; starting out with no qualifications, no money and following gut instinct. And then there's the whole range of stories in between.

There's no single way to become an entrepreneur. Anyone and everyone can acquire the enterprise skills that an entrepreneur needs even if they don't use them to set up and run businesses.

HOBSON'S CHOICE

Duncan Bannatyne seems to have had those enterprise skills from an early age and put them to good use when his local newsagent refused him his first paper round. And he put them to good use again when he seized the opportunity to buy his ice cream van. But leaving school without qualifications, getting kicked out of the Navy with a dishonourable discharge, getting arrested a few times and sent to jail once, all made him fairly unattractive to any prospective employer.

The truth may be that he couldn't work for anyone else given his dislike of authority or rules and regulations. So going into business was the obvious and only choice.

Bannatyne had another attribute essential for an entrepreneur: determination. He says he gets that from his father who, having been a prisoner of war, was determined to get fit, find a job and a wife, have children, and contribute to rebuilding the country he'd fought for. As a child Bannatyne was determined to be able to afford to buy his family ice cream, buy a bike, get his paper round and, even though he found school boring, pass his 11 plus and get into what the family called the 'posh school'. He did all of those things and always wanted more. He had that natural restlessness of the entrepreneur; always looking for the next move. And he realized that although he had taken his looks and determination from his father, he didn't want to grow up to be like him – leading the quiet family life, contented with his lot. Duncan couldn't get excited about the same things his father had.

There's no single way to become an entrepreneur.

But the famous Bannatyne determination wasn't consistent. At the 'posh school' he struggled, felt like a misfit and left without any qualifications. At 15 he was determined to get into the Navy but before long he was looking for a way out. He was dishonourably discharged at the age of 19 after a disagreement with his commanding officer. He told Lynn Barber in an interview for *The Observer* in 2007 that it was something he wasn't proud of but he wasn't particularly ashamed of it either. It had the desired result of getting him out of a situation he wasn't enjoying.

Bannatyne then spent years drifting, before the death of his oldest sister again gave him the determination to make something of himself. He sets a great deal of store on this event as a driving force in his life. He wonders aloud in the BBC *Dragons' Den* online video about how life would have been for him if his sister had lived and not made him the eldest in the family, but also wonders whether it was the fact that he only became the eldest later in life that kept him from becoming a successful entrepreneur sooner.

DETERMINED OR RUTHLESS?

Is Bannatyne always determined or sometimes just bloody minded? He's been called ruthless and arrogant, and over the years has gained a reputation for being a tough operator and hard-headed.

He argues that all entrepreneurs are arrogant to a certain extent – that you have to have that level of self-belief and belief in your ideas or you won't make them succeed. He suggests that he has swum with sharks and not been eaten alive and so merits the label 'tough operator' for standing by his principles and doing what's right for the business. Another attribute he has and believes every successful business person needs is common sense. But 'ruthless' is the label he disputes: 'I've worked with many of the most successful entrepreneurs of my generation ... and although we're all different we probably share a few key traits: we take responsibility for our actions, we are a pretty principled bunch (contrary to popular belief, very few of us are ruthless).' [2]

He can't have got where he's got without making some hard-headed decisions that had to be taken for the good of his businesses, like refusing to spend what he saw as excessive amounts of money. He's run a tight ship, demanded the resignation of people who felt they had the right to big expenses claims and sacked people who were ripping off his firms. There are undoubtedly disgruntled former employees and colleagues out there who would argue with Bannatyne's assessment of himself. But most of his longest serving and best performing managers are people he's nurtured over the years and who are loyal to the man.

So Bannatyne is the kind of businessman who does what has to be done to ensure the businesses flourish and make money. Anyone who uses common sense and determination, and is a tough operator, can do what he's done.

'You only learn about business by being in business': this is a phrase that Bannatyne repeats fairly frequently in his books and interviews. He is adamant that determination and common sense are much more use to a would-be entrepreneur than qualifications. Duncan Bannatyne didn't have experience or qualifications. Many of the most famous entrepreneurs in the UK may have millions in the bank and still don't have a qualification to their name – although a few do have honorary doctorates! (Bannatyne has two: a Doctorate in Science from the University of Glasgow and a Doctorate of Business Administration from the University of Teesside.)

He can't have got where he's got without making some hard-headed decisions that had to be taken for the good of his businesses.

Even with qualifications, you don't know what it's like to run a business until you start one yourself. You can read every business book ever written but that won't prepare you for doing it. By doing it you discover what natural attributes you bring to the table, what skills you have that you can use, what attributes you didn't know you had and skills that you'd forgotten you ever learned. Whether he recognized them or not, Bannatyne made up for lack of qualifications with natural business attributes – the attributes he used as a boy on a paper round and on the beaches of Jersey.

He points out that most successful entrepreneurs don't make money from their first business. They start a series of businesses, as he did, before they start the one that makes them rich. They learn as they go along and get the experience they need. With experience comes confidence. Sometimes some of their businesses fail, but eventually they accumulate enough experience, skills and confidence to make any business a success. Bannatyne gathered that experience from an early age and had probably gained far more experience than he imagined from buying, restoring and using cars for his early taxi business. In common with many UK entrepreneurs, he probably didn't even realize at that time he was in business.

One very practical and useful point that he reiterates from time to time in interviews is that whatever your business and whatever its size, there are leaflets and helplines to answer your questions. They take time to wade through but you can get through without qualifications. And if you do need people with specific qualifications for your businesses, such as the nurses Bannatyne needed for his care homes, you can employ them.

THE BUCK STOPS WITH YOU

While Bannatyne asserts that anyone can do what he did, he lays the blame for business failures firmly at the door of the people who start them up and run them. He says the main reason for most businesses failures is mistakes made by the boss and he cites two rules that he says all entrepreneurs must abide by if they're to succeed: they must work hard and be willing to accept responsibility for the business.

The kind of mistakes he talks about are a failure to do the market research and keep costs down; spending on the wrong things, often taking money out of a fledgling business for cars and bigger homes; hiring people who replicate your own skills rather than having complimentary skills; not listening to good advice in the first place; starting up when you weren't passionate about the business and not putting in the hard work it needed.

Capacity for hard work is certainly something Bannatyne has. He may work just five hours a week in his office now – but that wasn't always the case. Any business that he's started up seems to have taken over his life. He has put in the 18-hour days for months on end. Most entrepreneurs will tell you that you have to do that if that's what it takes.

'You only learn about business by being in business.'

At the beginning, entrepreneurs are likely to be doing everything like Bannatyne had to, unless they're starting up with a business partner or a team. There's the market research, the service or product to perfect, marketing, sales, customers to find and delight so they keep coming back, premises, admin, finances, and hiring staff. At the start-up stage, Bannatyne ended up doing the work of several people. It can get really tough and there's no option to take duvet days or call in sick. It's amazing how few sick days self-employed people take!

Bannatyne realized that it's vitally important that everyone an entrepreneur knows is backing them in their venture because personal relationships with family and friends, children and parents, or partners and pets often end up being left on the back burner. Sometimes people don't understand that and simmering resentment boils over into rows. Business ventures can result in relationship failure and the demands of partners can lead to business failure. Bannatyne was lucky that his first wife supported him when he was starting out, although they later parted.

That's the downside of the hard work. On a positive note, entrepreneurs learn all sorts of different skills and also discover a lot about themselves as Bannatyne did. When people are really passionate about an idea and their business, it's easier to put in the time and effort required. Bannatyne firmly believes that hiring the right people, trusting them and delegating with confidence is the key to enabling entrepreneurs to benefit from the success of their business or move on and look for the next venture.

Capacity for hard work is certainly something Bannatyne has.

So, according to Bannatyne, anyone can do it as long as they are determined, have common sense, work hard and take responsibility for their business. How you do it and how much of a success you make of it will depend on your own natural attributes, the skills you have to bring to the job, your contacts, your working environment and the team of people you build around you. Bannatyne can be quite glib when he talks about business in interviews, stressing how easy it is, and throwing in little asides about never having been given any useful advice. He seems to want to paint a picture of himself as someone to whom it all comes naturally; who found it all terribly easy, while making out that he's nothing special and just the same as the next person. He also comes across as impatient with the rest of humanity for failing to see and grasp the opportunities he sees all around him.

KNOCKING DOWN BARRIERS

How many times have you said (or heard someone you know say) 'I'd love to start my own business if only I had the time, the money, didn't have a big mortgage to pay, could afford to leave my job, had the qualifications, or had enough experience.' Bannatyne thinks what stops most people from going into business isn't really any of those things but the fear of failing. Maybe when you have nothing to lose – as he did – there are fewer barriers.

Work out what you need to earn to support a reasonable lifestyle. You may be giving up a well-paid job to get into business, but that doesn't mean you can expect to take out of the business what you have been earning. Equally, just because you've been earning a high salary doesn't mean that you can't afford to earn less. Be realistic.

At the beginning, entrepreneurs are likely to be doing everything unless they're starting up with a business partner or a team.

In Bannatyne's view, you shouldn't let lack of money stop you. He points out that there are plenty of businesses you can start which don't need much capital. You can work from home to keep your overheads down. If you need money for equipment or a van, save while you're still in a job or do what Bannatyne did to get his first nursing home opened up: sell things. You won't have time to watch TV anyway! There are grants and loans available for some businesses, and you may be able to raise money against the value of your home.

Bannatyne believes it always helps if you are running a business in something you are passionate about and believe in. You'll be happy to work hard, more inclined to take responsibility, interested to learn everything you can about the business and the sector, and all the more determined to succeed whatever the cost.

As Bannatyne discovered, you need to be careful about going into business with someone else. You need to work with someone who is as passionate about the business as you are. Most people don't need a business partner but if you do, it should be someone who complements the skills you bring rather than replicates them. Bannatyne did somewhat reluctantly go into his first care home with his neighbour, but since then – although he often employed the same people in his various projects – he set up his businesses on his own.

Entrepreneurs learn all sorts of different skills and also discover a lot about themselves.

Bannatyne had the support of his partner – it can keep you going when times get tough. If you're putting up money from savings, taking a risk with the family home, likely to be at work when you should be at a wedding, or bringing much less into the household while you get the business going, you need to discuss all those details with your other half. It can be easier running a business if you're single but it can be lonely.

ANYONE CAN DO IT

- **There's no single way to become a successful entrepreneur.** Bannatyne didn't worry about lack of qualifications – as long as you're determined and passionate about your idea, you can make your business work.
- **Many successful entrepreneurs didn't make money from the first or even second or third businesses.** Bannatyne learned about being in business by being in business, and it stood him in good stead for making a success of the next business he started up.
- **There are plenty of free sources of information available.** Bannatyne discovered that leaflets and helplines can answer your questions without the need to spend money.
- **As Bannatyne found out, at the beginning you'll be doing most of the different jobs in the business yourself.** You can't afford to be off sick and you need to be prepared to put in long hours.
- **Bannatyne takes responsibility for his businesses.** You can't blame the weather for the downturn in business! Stop looking for something to blame and start finding solutions.

2

KNOW YOURSELF AND FILL IN THE GAPS

'He has many of the characteristics of a Branson or Sugar. He's restless, direct, brutally honest and thoroughly determined – the archetype of an entrepreneur.'[1]

– Jon Card, growingbusiness.co.uk

Sometimes it's impossible to know what you're capable of until you've put yourself into a particular situation and tried yourself out. The old saying – often attributed to Eleanor Roosevelt, wife of President Franklin D. Roosevelt and human rights campaigner – 'a woman is like a teabag; you don't know how strong she is until she's in hot water' holds true. Just replace 'woman' with 'business owner'. But you can give yourself a head start by undergoing a business capability equivalent of an MOT.

PUTTING YOURSELF TO THE TEST

Duncan Bannatyne says that anyone can do what he's done and make £1 million or even £100 million. But to do so you need to be determined, apply common sense to your business and follow his two rules – work hard and take responsibility for your business. Beyond that there are several traits he mentions frequently that the ideal entrepreneur needs: be focused and see things through, be able to sell, be able to inspire your team, and be a good manager.

When you read an interview he's given about running a business, or watch him in action, it's clear that if Bannatyne were one of your customers, he'd expect you to know everything about your business. On *Dragons' Den* he expects business people looking for investment to have all the answers and be able to focus on all the different areas of business he asks them about, from the figures to the idea and the market for that idea. For an entrepreneur like Bannatyne there will be finance meetings with the bank manager, sales pitches with new clients, negotiations with suppliers, and discussions with staff about various aspects of how the business is operating and changes that might need to be made and all those aspects of the business require concentration and focus to get them right.

Bannatyne has the ability to focus on whatever aspect of his business he's dealing with at the time: that's how he avoids making mistakes. To focus effectively he has to know his business inside out and Bannatyne suggests it helps to write it all down – what excites you about the business and what you want out of it. That way you can remind yourself from time to time and make sure that you're still focused on what you set out to do.

Sometimes it's impossible to know what you're capable of until you've put yourself into a particular situation and tried yourself out.

Bannatyne is focused and passionate about his business and that helps him to see things through when times are difficult. If you aren't the kind of person who sees things through, your business will be in danger of failing. When the going gets tough in business there's always the temptation to throw in the towel and walk away. Bannatyne could have walked away from his ice cream business when he found it hadn't been well run while he was off caring for his wife, but he persevered and turned it around again. He could have walked away when he found it difficult to work with his neighbour, his partner in their first care home, but he learned the lesson and set up his next care home business by himself. If you're feeling like chucking it all in because it's too tough, Bannatyne suggests that's when you need to look at that piece of paper you've written to keep you focused.

Bannatyne has the advantage of being an ideas person as well as a 'doer'. He seems to see ideas everywhere he looks. Some people are the ideas people who get things off the ground and move on to the next venture leaving someone else in charge. Bannatyne has done that too. Now he has trusted teams to run his various businesses while he takes time with his family and *Dragons' Den*. However, he's still focused and in charge – so although someone else is doing the day-to-day stuff, he's still seeing the projects through.

BANNATYNE'S ADVICE

'Good salespeople make people happy.'[2] Bannatyne is a great salesperson. He suggests that anyone who runs a business is selling either their product or their service, and if you can't sell you won't convince customers to buy or investors to invest. When would-be entrepreneurs appear on *Dragons' Den*, they're selling their business idea to the Dragons. If the Dragons don't invest it's because the idea hasn't been successfully 'sold'. Bannatyne invests if a would-be entrepreneur successfully sells him their idea. He knows that if you make a sale you're happy, and if someone buys something they want or need then they're likely to be happy too. If no one buys into it, your business won't flourish – so if you aren't a salesperson, Bannatyne suggests that's possibly the first person you need to hire, or something you need to get some lessons on.

To focus effectively he has to know his business inside out

A really good point Bannatyne makes is that you must make sure you're talking to the right people – the wrong people won't be interested so you'll be wasting your time. He says in his books and in interviews that you will get rejections even if you're the world's best salesperson, but the more focused and passionate you are about your product or services, and the better you know the people you're talking to, the less the chance of rejection.

On top of that, Bannatyne has the passion and enthusiasm to sell his business ideas to his employees – to inspire them to be as confident in his plans as he is. For him it's vital that you are passionate about it and believe in it. If you can't believe in your business, how can you expect anyone else to? Ultimately, people are investing in you. If you can inspire passion and belief in others too, they'll be with you all the way. The Bannatyne impatience and frustration with people who don't live up to this is there for all to see on *Dragons' Den*, just before another declaration of 'I'm out'.

There's plenty of computer software to help with cash and data systems, but people are a different matter.

Bannatyne believes that one thing that inspires people is good management. If they can see a business is well run, from the cash flow systems and data storage, and they feel that you're good with people too, they'll be inspired about the business. There's plenty of computer software to help with cash and data systems, but people are a different matter. Some bosses can manage one or the other but not both. Bannatyne is good at the figures but says himself that he is less good with people and happy to leave their management to others. Yet he instinctively understands the need to build a good team around him, to delegate to the members of that team according to their strengths and skills and leave them to get on with their own jobs. A Bannatyne mantra is: 'delegate, delegate'.

But that's not all you need to succeed. As well as the capacity for hard work, taking responsibility for his businesses and having the above traits at his fingertips, Bannatyne has various other skills and experiences to which his success can be attributed.

YOU SWOT

There are all sorts of tests to help you work out what your natural business attributes are. One of them is the SWOT test, which Bannatyne is a fan of. It's a well-used business technique that you can apply to yourself in much the same way you would to your business idea or business plan. A SWOT test is an in-depth check of your strengths, weaknesses, opportunities and threats. If you can identify strengths like good leadership or management skills, a real flair for selling, or being the person who is always coming up with great ideas, you can build a business that plays to those strengths and find other people to do the parts of the job that you're weak at.

Talking to other people who know you well can help you to identify forgotten skills.

Bannatyne gives the impression in his books of being in favour of orthodox business methods, but at the same time he seems to feel that it's his very lack of traditional business training that gives him his edge.

One of Bannatyne's strengths seems to lie in spotting opportunities for businesses. He seems to be restless, always looking for the next deal or project. That restlessness is one of the reasons he's great at coming up with ideas and setting things up, and makes him move on while others to carry on what he's started. So restlessness could be said to be both a strength and a weakness. Another of Bannatyne's strengths seems to be in building effective teams who can pick the businesses up and keep them working after he's moved on.

Bannatyne knows himself well. He suggests that that's very important if you want to succeed in business and that another useful way of working out what you bring to the business is to talk to the people who know you best: former employers, colleagues, long-term friends, relations. Given permission to be honest, they'll be happy to help you identify your strengths and weaknesses! They'll tell you whether you are great at thinking outside the box or are a maverick who's difficult to work with! As Bannatyne knows, it can be a painful exercise, but sometimes more useful than a self-assessment where we can cheat to get the desired outcome.

Even if you're a one-person band with no employees, you can build a team of people who are important to your business.

SKILLS

Despite leaving school without any qualifications Bannatyne recognized that he had skills he could bring to his businesses. Over the years – in the Navy, in Jersey as an ice cream seller, restoring his cars and driving taxis – he was honing his business skills, particularly his selling and customer care skills.

He appreciates that people may have qualifications such as plumber or lawyer, but there will be other skills they've acquired through running the local football team or PTA, speaking at the historical society, or selling on an auction site. They're all things that can be put to good use in a business – just as Bannatyne embellished his ice creams or recognized what his customers would want. You get your skills through qualifications, work, home, hobbies or sport and, as he points out, there will be lots you've forgotten about. Talking to other people who know you well can help you to identify forgotten skills.

YOUR NETWORK

Bannatyne says he's always been too single-minded to look for much help from his network of friends, business acquaintances and colleagues, but he stresses that they are an important aspect of business. People often say despairingly that it's a case of 'who you know, not what you know' that's important. It's usually said about someone who's been successful despite having few skills and positive attributes!

You can find useful contacts through research and recommendations – suppliers, advisers. But Bannatyne suggests you'll already know people who can help because of their own experiences or relevant contacts. Using them to get things moving faster is networking. People who set up in business work very hard and can feel quite isolated.

Bannatyne suggests that one of the most valuable members of a team is a mentor.

A strong network can also give you support when you're struggling and feeling like walking away. Bannatyne points out that people like being asked for their advice. It makes them feel important and useful. He advocates having a look through your list of contacts to see if anyone you already know might be able to help. If you identify someone from outside your network who could help, see if you can get a personal introduction. Bannatyne believes that there should be something in every deal for each party involved, so it also helps if you can offer something in return – even if it is at a later date. Treat your contacts with the same respect you would you family and friends.

ONE LAST THING

Bannatyne knows that even if you're a one-person band with no employees, you can build a team of people who are important to your business. Ideally they'll have all the attributes and skills between them that you wish you had yourself. If you can't employ them, look for friends, relations and advisers who have what you're missing and turn to them for help.

Bannatyne suggests that one of the most valuable members of a team is a mentor. Think of someone you've worked for, or with, who you respect, and whose opinions and experience you'd like to tap into, and ask them to be part of your team, challenging your assumptions and giving you a different perspective on you business.

KNOW YOURSELF AND FILL IN THE GAPS

- **Be passionate about the business.** Bannatyne believes in his ventures, knows them inside out, and isn't just motivated by money.
- **Take responsibility for the business** and don't make excuses – come up with solutions. It's one of Bannatyne's top rules.
- **Do a reality check** and work out what your natural attributes and weaknesses are. Bannatyne knows himself well.
- **Identify a range of skills** that you can use in their business. Bannatyne acquired many useful skills along the way.
- **Manage, inspire, sell, focus and see things through as Bannatyne does.** You will need a network of useful contacts, and the space and time to work and think
- **Use a team of people** – either employees and friends or mentors – who have the attributes and skills to fill in the gaps. Bannatyne believes in delegating to the right people.

3

THE RIGHT IDEAS ARE EVERYWHERE YOU LOOK

'In my experience, I've found that simplicity often brings success in business and that the most profitable ideas are uncomplicated solutions to everyday problems.'[1]

– Duncan Bannatyne

Many people claim they'd love to run their own business, but they're not ideas people. You don't have to come up with the next 'internet' to start up in business. Inventors do occasionally come up with things we all eventually come to think of as essentials, like fridges and mobile phones, but a lot of 'terrific new ideas' fall by the wayside because they won't create a viable business. And most businesses are based on existing ideas.

GIVE IT A NEW SPIN

For someone who claims to be a maverick – dictionary definition: 'dissenter, who takes an independent stand apart from his or her associates' – it's ironic that Bannatyne seems almost proud to admit that he's never had an original idea for a business in his life. All of his businesses are based on ventures already run by others. His independence comes with his determination to give those ideas an original element. He started up his health clubs in towns where there wasn't one already and his nurseries in areas were there weren't enough places for all the children who needed them.

Many people claim they'd love to run their own business, but they're not ideas people.

Another Bannatyne mantra is that if you do copy someone else's idea, you should improve on it. His nursing homes were among the first in the UK to have private rooms with their own toilets. It was something other care home providers hadn't thought about and made a place in one of his Quality Care Homes very desirable. His philosophy seems to be that thinking about how you can make a business better will motivate you to prove you're the best in your field and help you to steal market share from your rivals.

SOLVE A PROBLEM

Bannatyne is also a great advocate of 'Wouldn't it be great if ...?' ideas. Wouldn't it be great if you had a vacuum cleaner that didn't have a bag to be changed? Wouldn't if be great if you could have exactly the right amount of hot water for a cup of tea without boiling too much in the kettle? Sometimes these are ideas that make small improvements on something that's already on the market and sometimes they are quite revolutionary, but they work because they provide customers with goods or services that they need.

Bannatyne points out that the entrepreneurs who struggle are often those who copy others' ideas without doing the research to find out if there are enough customers to go around or if the market is already saturated. Just because there are ten busy hairdressers in one small town doesn't mean that there are enough customers to make an eleventh a viable business. But the eleventh might succeed if it gives customers something that they need that the others don't. Or it might succeed because it brings to the area a technique that local people currently travel to the nearest big town to buy.

SEE THE WOOD FOR THE TREES

Bannatyne sees ideas everywhere: on radio and TV, in the pub, in the papers, in the street when you're out and about. It's about recognizing them as possible business ideas, looking for where there is a gap in the sector, or finding a way to add value to what exists already.

This seems to be the key to Duncan Bannatyne's success. He can spot opportunities and find the gap in the market. He seems to have difficulty understanding why other people don't see the opportunities that he does, but he really does seem to have the kind of mind that is constantly, and probably subconsciously, looking for opportunities. Is he a successful serial entrepreneur because he naturally has that opportunity-seeking mind, or does he have that mindset because he had nothing to lose and needed to spot the opportunities? Either way, he's constantly on the lookout for the next thing.

All of his businesses are based on ventures already run by others.

Bannatyne's Director of Projects, Tony Bell, who has worked with him since the days of Quality Care Homes, thinks that his boss's success is down to his lack of formal training. If that's the case, he's more likely to see the wood for the trees, because he follows his instincts. Bannatyne himself seems to think that if he'd had a good job he wouldn't have become a millionaire because he wouldn't have followed those instincts. Whether or not that's true is impossible to tell, but with his natural entrepreneurial attributes it's unlikely a job would ever have been enough. And as we've already seen from his Navy days he doesn't like taking orders!

FOR 'CHANGE' READ 'OPPORTUNITY'

Bannatyne had the idea for his chain of nursing homes while watching television. It was early in the 1980s and the government announced that it would pay £140 a week for each patient in residential or £260 for those in nursing care. He worked out that if he had fifty residents, he'd have a guaranteed turnover of £7000 a week. Apparently he does these 'back-of-a-fag-packet' calculations, as he calls them, at a very early stage with each business idea to check that it can be turned from idea into viable business.

A bit of research led to the discovery that the government produces leaflets on everything you ever needed to know about business and legislation. A big hotel came up for sale in Scarborough that could be converted into individual residences and it became the forerunner of Bannatyne's Quality Care Homes chain. Other people were already providing care, so the idea wasn't new, but Bannatyne set out to improve on what was already on offer and came up with en suite facilities for each room. Wouldn't it be great if … care home residents didn't have to share toilets!

Other people were already providing care, so the idea wasn't new, but Bannatyne set out to improve on what was already on offer.

The idea to open a health club came to Bannatyne as a result of having to drive half an hour from home to a gym that had the right equipment to help him rebuild his knee muscles after a skiing accident. He had a fair idea that if he didn't want to drive that far to find a gym, others would prefer not to either. If something would make your life easier, the chances are that there are other people who would appreciate it too. So Bannatyne opened a gym near his home. When he couldn't find a nursery for two of his daughters, he had the idea of opening a daycare centre for children. There were nurseries already, but obviously not enough places for all the people who needed them.

As shown from these few examples, Bannatyne certainly seems to have the knack of understanding how to give people what they need to make their lives easier. In his business book *Wake Up and Change Your Life*, Bannatyne lists the financial pages, the trade press, local papers, your hobbies and your current employment, as well as moaning friends, as good sources of ideas. He suggests that you look at what you do now as an employee and think of how you can turn your expertise into a business to rival your employer, perhaps thinking how you could improve on what your boss offers. If you're tempted to do that, read your contract to see whether there's any restriction on where and when you can set up a rival business!

He also swears by using your eyes. While you're out and about, look for queues, look at the people you meet, look at businesses that haven't moved with the times or are in the wrong location, and look at what's missing. He found his first hotel in Darlington while driving around the town with his partner (later to become his second wife) Joanne McCue, looking for something in which to invest the money he'd made from selling his care homes.

SWOT UP ON YOUR IDEA

With so many ideas floating around, how on earth do you choose what to follow up and what to drop? Duncan Bannatyne seems very keen on the SWOT test, as we saw in the previous chapter. He uses it on new ideas and his existing businesses. He advocates that you do a very thorough analysis of the strengths and weaknesses of your idea and look at the opportunities to make it work and at the threats it faces. There's no such a thing as a standard set of questions to ask yourself in the SWOT test; that depends on the nature of your business. Talk it over with someone who knows what your idea is and their questions will help you.

SMOULDERING PASSION

Bannatyne believes that the best businesses are started when the founder's skills fit the opportunity. But he says you must ask

EXAMPLES OF STRENGTHS, WEAKNESSES, OPPORTUNITIES AND THREATS

- **Strengths:** Your service or product is better than any of your rivals; you have a lot of expertise; it's something new that people need.
- **Weaknesses:** The business is vulnerable (to the weather, for example); you don't have much experience; it's hard to get good staff; customers are likely to need your product or service only once; the prices are too high.
- **Opportunities:** You can see a good chance to get more customers or charge more; the area is changing in some way that means more people will want your service; there's a supplier who will give you a better deal.
- **Threats:** You have rivals who can afford to undercut you; your costs are rising but your customers can't afford to pay more; once the property market recovers fewer people will want your product; it would be easy for someone to copy your idea.

yourself whether the business is right for you: feeling passionate about it is one of the most important tell-tale signs. After all, you're going to have to work at it very hard and, possibly, for years, so if you're not passionate about it you're likely to be miserable. If it will make you a reasonable income, make you happy and fit your skills (or you can hire someone with the right skills), and if you think your business can be the business of your dreams and it really gets your mind racing, then it's right for you.

Never underestimate the amount of hard work you'll need to put in to get it running smoothly and if you aren't passionate about the business and it doesn't make you happy you won't put in the necessary graft. When Bannatyne discovered that he hated being covered in oil, he bailed out of the garage he was running in Jersey. He shows that it's important not to get hung up on failure. You'll have learned a lot about yourself, and about what does make you passionate and happy, and there may be even bigger opportunities around the corner.

Never underestimate the amount of hard work you'll need to put in to get it running smoothly.

If a business isn't right for you, Bannatyne says it's better to know that before you spend a lot of money on it. Walk away. But he points out that even though the business isn't right for you, you might be able to make some money out of your idea. Think about whether someone who already works in that field might pay you for it. If it's something that will save them money, help them beat their competition, cut their costs or attract more customers, there could be money in it for you too. Bannatyne belatedly realized that when he was a boy and collected a list of 100 households that would like a newspaper delivered every day, he could have sold it to the newsagent instead of taking on the paper round himself. It's one of the few business mistakes he admits to.

Bannatyne is the master of the art of spotting ideas and working out whether or not to run with them. He can and does walk away if he isn't convinced that he's going to make a reasonable return on his investment. As he often says on *Dragons' Den*: 'it isn't a business, I'm out.' He isn't necessarily rejecting the idea as a bad one; he just isn't convinced that a business based on that idea will be a viable one. That's something he's learned by being in business. Ideas are just the start of the process and only a small part of it. It's the execution that makes the business successful.

RED TAPE GOOD!

Several of Duncan Bannatyne's business ventures have been launched off the back of changes to government legislation. Even before the nursing homes were built a government initiative had made him money. When he was running his ice cream business in Stockton he was also buying and doing up terraced houses to let out. When the government announced in 1979 that it would pay £46 a week direct to landlords to cover the rent of people who were out of work and on benefit, Bannatyne saw that as an opportunity.

He turned his terraced houses into bedsits and the rent for all of those bedsit tenants was paid straight to him. Some landlords didn't like to take unemployed benefit claimants and missed the opportunity. When the law changed again and the money for rent was paid to the tenants, Bannatyne was less keen – but by then he was selling off his houses to fund his first care home. Red tape can have its advantages.

ONE LAST THING

People often worry that if they talk about their business idea someone else will steal it, but most people are too wrapped up in themselves and their own businesses to steal yours. Bannatyne argues that you'll miss a great opportunity to test your idea out on other people if you keep quiet about it and that there is more to be gained by speaking to people than keeping it a secret.

If you have come up with something truly innovative, the Intellectual Property Office will talk you through whether it's something you can get a patent on. You can't patent an idea but you can apply for a patent on a new piece of working technology if it's different enough from existing technology. Other possible lines of defence are trademarks and intellectual property rights. These are very complex areas of law that the Intellectual Property Office can help you with too.

THE RIGHT IDEAS ARE EVERYWHERE YOU LOOK

- **Just because you have a good idea doesn't mean you can make it into a good business.** Bannatyne sees ideas everywhere, but knows that the idea is a very small part; the rest is hard work.
- **Make sure you have the Bannatyne passion for the idea** to put in the hard work that will be needed.
- **Road-test the idea on anyone who will listen.** If they all tell you it's something that would solve a problem for them or make their lives easier, or it's something they need, Bannatyne says you may be on to a winner. If some of them are enthusiastic, think carefully about who they are and why they're interested while others aren't. They may be your target market.
- **Do an in-depth SWOT test** and a back-of-a-fag-packet calculation, and try out the competition. Bannatyne does all three.

- **Make sure you have all the skills and contacts you need**, or that you can employ someone else who has.
- **Act decisively.** If the idea will translate into a business that will make you happy, fit in with your lifestyle, make you the income you're looking for, and be the business of your dreams, Bannatyne believes that you have to move quickly before someone else gets in there and grabs the customers. If all that checking and double-checking convinces you that the business isn't right for you, walk away or try to sell your idea to someone who can make it work.
- **Bannatyne advocates that you don't need to spend a lot of money at the ideas stage on lawyers or accountants:** there's a free government leaflet on just about everything you'll need to know or you can find it on the internet. The government's business advice services – Business Link in England and Wales, Business Gateway in Scotland and nibusinessinfo.co.uk in Northern Ireland – are terrific free resources.

4

DON'T SKIMP ON THE RESEARCH

'Founders don't do enough research. In my view this probably accounts for most business failures.'[1]

– Duncan Bannatyne

From hotels and fitness to children's nurseries and radio stations, Duncan Bannatyne has made a success of them all. While he doesn't always follow the conventional rules of business, he does set a great deal of store by research. He's a master of the art of 'spotting a gap in the market' but he knows that without the science of research, there's no way of telling whether there is viable business to be made out of plugging that gap.

GETTING TO KNOW THE ICE CREAM TRADE

Ice cream was a growing business in 1979. The famous Ice Cream Wars in Glasgow were still a few years off, violence between rival vendors over lucrative pitches was still rare and there was money to be made in ice cream. Bannatyne's research around the Stockton-on-Tees area showed that there was a gap in the market because there was still room for another operator. His research also showed him that he could do ice cream differently and better, and win over a big enough share of the market from existing operators to make his business viable.

Soft ice cream was popular with customers and with vendors, because it could be served quickly to long queues on hot summer days. Bannatyne researched suppliers and discovered that he couldn't make enough money selling the big brands like Wall's because he couldn't charge his customers enough to make a reasonable profit. The traditional 'hard' ice cream he sourced was more difficult to serve, but Bannatyne then sought out an ice cream scoop from the US that was easier and quicker to use than the mashed potato scoop most vendors used for hard ice cream. He could keep up with his rivals.

The new scoop left a mark on the top of the ice cream like a smile and he filled the lips with strawberry sauce and used aniseed balls for eyes. The children were hooked. The added value allowed him to add two pence to the price and guaranteed him longer queues. He named his creations after the Muppets and the children became discerning customers, demanding 'the smoking frog' – a Kermit with a 99 Flake.

Continued perusal of the local papers threw up another opportunity. He bought a concession to guarantee that he would be a park's only ice cream vendor and went on to build up his fleet of vans to six.

RESEARCH WITH CARE

When it came to setting up his new nursing homes, Bannatyne visited existing homes on the pretext of looking for a place for his mother. He says he was shocked by what he saw and was grateful his mother didn't need a care place. He found elderly ladies living six to a room and using commodes because there weren't enough staff and toilet facilities. He vowed to make a difference and to provide facilities people would want to use and that would improve their lives.

His nursing homes came with individual rooms, most of which had en suite toilets. When he headhunted a senior member of staff from an existing care home operator, she was convinced that most of the elderly people she already worked with would want to move with her to a Quality Care Home. Bannatyne prides himself on having changed the way elderly people were cared for in the UK.

His next venture was children's nurseries. Other people were running nurseries but Bannatyne again applied his principle of adding value and doing it better than his rivals. He saw that where you have children, they need toilet facilities and staff to help them use those facilities. If the toilets are close to the children, and convenient for the staff, and each room opens out onto the playground, supervision is much easier and fewer staff are required. So that's what Just Learning, his nursery business, did. Bannatyne spotted the need for more nurseries with that kind of 'added value' when he tried to find nursery places for his own daughters. No nursery could take them both, so he recognized a shortage of spaces and a gap in the market.

While he doesn't always follow the conventional rules of business, he does set a great deal of store by research.

FIGHTING FIT

When it came to setting up his biggest venture, Bannatyne Health and Leisure (which later became Bannatyne Fitness), the idea was inspired by a skiing accident in France. Once he had been released from hospital he spent a lot of time building up his fitness again in local gyms. There he did his research.

What he saw led him to believe that he could build a chain of health and leisure centres – again, not a new idea, but he thought he could do it better. He built facilities near where people lived so they could cut down on their travel, and gyms that were suitable for couples to work out together. Constant research into who used his clubs and when led him to the conclusion, for example, that if cars were queuing to get into the car park at a particular time, he needed more car parking space.

Bannatyne advocates ongoing research among existing customers by asking their views and listening to their complaints. One woman's concern led to the provision of family changing rooms in Bannatyne clubs. She felt uncomfortable changing in front of another woman's eight-year-old son – partly because she was his teacher. Doing constant research meant that Bannatyne was able to take the lessons learned from each club into each new club opened, just as lessons from previous businesses are taken into new ventures.

Bannatyne prides himself on having changed the way elderly people were cared for in the UK.

In 2006 Bannatyne bought out the Living Well chain of 25 clubs owned by the Hilton Hotel Group, making Bannatyne Fitness the biggest independent fitness chain in the UK. The two chains had different business cultures and a lot of staff left because they didn't like the way the new boss changed things. But small changes that had worked for his original fitness clubs, such as turnstiles at the entrance to stop people getting in without paying, immediately pushed up profits.

RESEARCH THE COMPETITION

Once you've got your idea, Bannatyne says initial research will tell you whether or not it's worth following it up. Find out who else is doing what you'd like to do. If you haven't been in business before, or haven't done business in a particular sector, the chances are you won't know everyone involved or what they provide.

Imagine you are trying to buy the product or service for yourself. Do everything you'd normally do when shopping around. Ask anyone and everyone to recommend people doing what you're intending to offer. The more difficult they find it to come up with suggestions, the more chance there's room for your business. Bannatyne uses the phone book, newspapers, trade magazines and search engines, and shops for it on the internet. Check out your rivals' accounts through Companies House to see how well they're doing.

Bannatyne advocates ongoing research among existing customers by asking their views and listening to their complaints.

If you find that there are already people doing what you want to do, Bannatyne says that it doesn't always mean there isn't room for you too. Pretend to be a customer and check out your rivals' product or service and prices, as Bannatyne did when he visited existing care homes. As he warns, other people may already be doing everything you want to do at competitive prices that you can't undercut, so you may have to accept that there's no room for you in the market and you have no business. If they have more work than they can cope with, though, there's space in the market for another operator. If you can do it better – perhaps in a more up-to-date way, with added value or at better prices in a more convenient location – you may well be onto a winner.

RESEARCH THE CUSTOMERS

Who will want to buy what you want to offer? And how many of those who want your service or product will become customers? They're familiar questions to anyone who watches Bannatyne in action on *Dragons' Den*. He wants to know that you'll have enough customers to make a business.

You can get information from the last census to help you work out how many of your target customers are in your area. If you want to sell from a shop, you need passing trade – so spend some time in the premises you're thinking of using, watching the people walking past. Check out how easy it would be for customers to park.

For his fitness centres Bannatyne uses a market research agency to do what he calls 'a ten-minute drive time analysis' of the potential location. This is based on his calculation that people don't want to drive more than ten minutes for a workout. The idea is to draw a circle around a potential venue that includes all the people who are a ten-minute drive away from it; the agency checks out how many of his target customers live within the circle. If there aren't enough, he drops the plan and moves on. If there are, he carries on with his research.

Once you've got your idea, Bannatyne says initial research will tell you whether or not it's worth following it up.

When a health club came up for sale in Leith Docks in Edinburgh, it occurred to Bannatyne that there was a big market of young professional people who might use it. But when he did his ten-minute drive time analysis, it was obvious that half of his circle was in the sea – so his potential customer base was halved.

Market research companies use all sorts of methods to work out how many potential customers you could attract, such as surveys and focus groups. But this can also be done without having to pay an agency's fees. Bannatyne says you can come up with a questionnaire asking people what they think about your business idea, what they'd want from it and whether they'd use it – and ask everyone you email it to to forward it to their contacts.

THE CUSTOMERS ARE OUT THERE – NOW REACH FOR THEM

As Bannatyne points out, just because hundreds of thousands of babies are born every year, creating hundreds of thousands of potential customers for a nappy laundering service, that doesn't mean they're going to buy *your* nappy laundering service.

Bannatyne reached his care home target customers through local authorities and hospitals that needed homes for their patients. He filled up his gyms by offering discount joining and membership deals. His nurseries were a different matter, because parents didn't want to move their children from their existing nursery as they'd be separated from their friends. That meant finding a new way, so they offered care for babies and built up the business as more babies were born.

Advertising is expensive, something that fledgling businesses often can't afford, and may not get cost-effective results – so Bannatyne says your research needs to include ways of letting your potential customers know about your business and what it can do for them. Articles in the local press or radio and TV are great if you can generate them. Sometimes pushing good old-fashioned fliers through letterboxes is the best way.

A LACK OF RESEARCH CAN COST YOU DEAR

Bannatyne puts one of his failures down to not doing enough research. Lady in Leisure was a women-only gym he'd come across while researching his health and leisure business. He was asked to join the board and bought shares, only to discover that the business wasn't being run well. The company was listed on AIM, the Alternative Investment Market for small businesses.

Lady In Leisure was small, but he reckoned the directors were living the high life with big offices and flash cars. Instead of walking away, as he admits other investors might have done, he bought more shares. His aim was to own 10% of the company and have enough clout with the board to force through changes. He had his eye on an eventual takeover.

Market research companies use all sorts of methods to work out how many potential customers you could attract.

With his 10% in his top pocket, Bannatyne called for an extraordinary AGM and the resignation of the managing director. The board agreed to discuss the MD's resignation but then refused to accept it. When they subsequently went back to the stock market to raise another £3 million, Bannatyne resigned. His total investment was just over £1 million and a year later Lady in Leisure went bust. He lost the lot, all due to a lack of research at the outset.

When the administrators for Lady in Leisure eventually came back to Bannatyne a couple of years later, to ask if he was still interested in taking over the company, he declined the offer. His research had convinced him that 'Ladies' don't want to work out in women-only clubs; many couples prefer to work out together. It was an expensive lesson learned the hard way.

DON'T SKIMP ON THE RESEARCH

- **Talk to people about the business idea.** Bannatyne says their reactions will tell you whether or not there may be custom for it. (But allow for the 'mum' factor … mums tend to think that everything their offspring suggest is brilliant.)
- **It can be a hard slog**, costing time and effort before the business is even off the ground. But Bannatyne says it's better to know, before spending a lot of hard-earned cash, if there's no market for a particular product or service.
- **If you're not borrowing to set up or expand, your own research efforts may be enough.** But lenders and investors will want to know what the research shows about the viability of the business. As an investor, Bannatyne is not going to lend unless he's convinced it will have the customers it needs to succeed. It's at that stage that a market research company can be worth its research fees.
- **More research is needed at every stage of the business's development.** By doing this, you will find the best location for a new shop or hotel, or to identify a market for a new product.
- **Do free research, Bannatyne-style.** Visit the competition and use free government materials.
- **Customers are an invaluable source of information.** Build systems like Bannatyne did at his fitness centres to allow you to collect that information for research purposes. In other words, ask them what changes and products or services they would welcome and ask their permission to write down and keep what they say in your database.
- **Every new idea needs its own research** but you learn about business by being in business, as Bannatyne did, so experience can be applied to each new idea.

5

PLAN YOUR ENTERPRISE

'I like business plans to start with an "elevator pitch" – basically what you would say to Bill Gates, or me, if you bumped into us in the lift and had only ten seconds to convince us not to get out at the next floor.'[1]

– Duncan Bannatyne

Although Duncan Bannatyne claims to rely on gut instinct and to be a bit of a maverick, he is clearly someone who does his planning. From his initial 'back-of-a-fag-packet' calculations, to the full-blown business plan he presents to the bank manager, there's little evidence to back up his claim that he's not hot on detail. But then again, he does admit that he's got a brilliant team of people around him who are good at sketching out business plans quickly.

Whoever does it, the planning seems to pay off. Even if he doesn't come away from a meeting with the bank manager, having convinced them to put up all the money he wants to get a particular project off the ground, Bannatyne does seem to have plans in place that are viable. Having said that, he does also claim that once its done its job, he never looks at a business plan again!

THE QUICK CALCULATION

When you see Bannatyne and the other Dragons scribbling in their notebooks during a pitch in *Dragons' Den*, they're doing a quick calculation to see whether or not they think a business is financially viable. No matter how brilliant the idea is, the first question has to be 'can this idea make a business?' If their initial workings out don't add up, there's no business and they won't invest. Sometimes they suggest selling the idea to an existing business. That way, you'd get some money for the idea and the firm that bought it would be able to make it make money where you wouldn't. Everyone wins. Otherwise you struggle to get your brilliant idea to market and lose money along the way.

Bannatyne's calculation includes a rough estimate of all his costs and income to see if it's worthwhile taking the idea any further. The research he's already done allows him to make a fair stab at the figures. Put simply, all he wants to know is how much it will cost to produce the product, how much it can be charged for and how many customers it would create. With all those figures to hand, Bannatyne says if you aren't feeling something akin to real love for your project, it's time to make the choice: forget it or rethink it to make it better.

Although Duncan Bannatyne claims to rely on gut instinct and to be a bit of a maverick, he is clearly someone who does his planning.

THE SENSITIVITY TEST

One thing Bannatyne is very keen on is what's known in business as a sensitivity analysis. It's accountancy speak for working out how sensitive a business would be to rising costs and falling sales. Bannatyne advocates asking 'what if?' questions. 'What if I've underestimated my costs?' 'What if my sales are lower than I expect?'

This is a way of checking whether the business can still make money if his figures are out. An entrepreneur should adjust costs and sales figures by 10%, then 20%, and so on, and see how much of a change they could withstand and still make money.

He does the same kind of calculation on his cash flow to find out how difficult it would be to stay in business if interest rates went up on any loans he takes out.

THE BIG PLAN

If you've done all your initial calculations, they've stood up to scrutiny and you're passionate about your business, it's time to do the plan. People sometimes claim not to have done any kind of plan. Bannatyne claims he had never done one until he and his bank manager did one together when he needed a loan for his first nursing home. Businesses that don't need loans or investors probably don't in theory need one, but it usually helps to have something in writing to guide you from time to time. It's helpful to have the aims of the business written down, if nothing else, so you can keep reminding yourself of why you set it up in the first place. Very few businesses don't benefit from a written plan.

There's no 'right' way to make a business plan. There's plenty of help on the internet and from Business Link, the government's free business advice service. Advisers can help you with your plans for free. Bannatyne is in the position where he gets business plans regularly from people who want him to invest in their businesses. He appeals to would-be entrepreneurs to refrain from doing anything out of the ordinary with the format, such as eye-catching fonts and strange layouts. He gives a lot of advice in his books, but basically his view is that it's the substance, not the style, that's important; you should give it to a friend to read, to see it they can make sense of it; and keep refining it until your message is crystal clear.

PLANNING THE BANNATYNE BUSINESS EMPIRE

Bannatyne's second business venture – a residential care home with a neighbour as his business partner – involved buying a six-storey hotel in Scarborough with planning permission to turn it into a residential home for the elderly. It took several months to raise the finance but it wasn't until the business was up and running and he'd decided to build his own nursing home that he was faced with the prospect of having to write a business plan.

Bannatyne did his research, checked out the competition by pretending to be looking for a home for his mother, found out about all the relevant rules and regulations from government leaflets, and found a plot of land for sale. It already had the planning permission he needed. He put his house up as security for the £25,000 he needed to borrow to buy the land.

Bannatyne's calculation includes a rough estimate of all his costs and income to see if it's worthwhile taking the idea any further.

But the same bank wouldn't lend him the money to build the home. After trying a few other banks for the money, he found one that liked to say yes. The manager needed a business plan. Bannatyne had never heard of one before and asked the bank manager to help him write it.

They took his basic figures of 'so many residents at so much a week', subtracted the predicted costs of running the place and came up with a plan that convinced the lenders. Bannatyne didn't find it hard to write the plan because he found all the figures fairly straightforward, but he felt it was an interesting exercise. He discovered that banks are – in his opinion – risk-averse and began to understand how they view new ventures.

Despite the effort that went into that business plan, Bannatyne didn't get his money immediately. He had to fund the building of the nursing home himself. The bank promised him a 70% mortgage once it was built and fully occupied by elderly residents. He sold everything he owned, including his car and TV, ran up credit card debts, sold the ice cream business, and eventually agreed to pay his builder 10% a month interest on the money he owed him if he'd wait for payment until the nursing home was completed. Only after the bank manager had visited the completed home and seen with his own eyes 30 rooms and 30 elderly people (some of them friends of Bannatyne's mother who were bussed in for the day) did Bannatyne get his money.

DO AS I SAY, DON'T DO AS I DO!

Bannatyne says he never looked at that business plan for his first nursing home again. Most business advisers would suggest that you don't leave your business plan unloved in the back of a drawer.

Very few businesses don't benefit from a written plan.

If nothing else, a plan can be a kind of road map: if you take a look at it regularly you'll be able to see how you're progressing. But it's a living document and as things change in the business, the plan needs to develop accordingly. You can add information as you get it. As your business develops you'll learn new things and may decide to change the direction of your business; the plan needs to change too. You can change it to make it more relevant to the people you intend sending it to, depending on the kind of information they're likely to want. It is often the first piece of information an investor will have come across about your business, so it needs to be as impressive as you can make it but at the same time clear and understandable.

Whether or not Bannatyne ever looks at a business plan again, it's fairly certain that he's running it constantly through his mind.

He may not be good on details and leaves that to others, but he's always looking for ways to run his business more dynamically and that's another way of saying he's forever planning.

WHAT INVESTORS LOOK FOR IN A PLAN

Even if Bannatyne delegates the planning to his team, that doesn't stop him expecting others, who approach him for investment, to have a well-laid plan! If you're going into business for the first time you may be in the same position as Bannatyne was and have had no reason to have experience of business plans. It's like most things in business: there's no right or wrong way to draw one up, but there are certain things any investor (including the bank manager) will want to know about your business.

A plan can be a kind of road map: if you take a look at it regularly you'll be able to see how you're progressing.

Bannatyne likes business plans to start with what he calls the 'elevator pitch', which says in a snappy way what you do. It needs to be catchy and tell him the basic premise clearly and concisely. If a potential investor like Bannatyne doesn't 'get it' in the opening paragraph, you'll have lost them altogether. As he points out, it can be difficult to fit your vision into one catchy sentence – but it focuses the mind. In the rest of the document, Bannatyne wants to see all the reasons why someone is convinced their business is a winner and worth backing. He wants to know that what you're planning will give him a reasonable return on his money.

And he's not alone. Investors aren't being greedy: they're in business and business is all about making money. He wants you to spell out how the business will make money, who the customers will be, how many of them you will attract, what the return on his investment will be, what the turnover and profits will be over the next few years, and why you're the best person to make the business work. Investors like Bannatyne want to know you've done your research and your business has a market to tap into – otherwise, 'they're out'.

He's always looking for ways to run his business more dynamically and that's another way of saying he's forever planning.

If you think about how Bannatyne and his colleagues on *Dragons' Den* operate, they want all that information. One of Bannatyne's most regularly used phrases is 'It's not a business; I'm out.' What he means is that the person presenting the pitch hasn't convinced him that the business will make enough money, have enough customers, or that they're the right person to invest in. For Bannatyne, the person seems to be important. He occasionally says 'I like you, so I'll invest' when other Dragons drop out. If he likes the person pitching and believes in them, he'll be more inclined to see how the business can operate and that it's worth taking the risk – but Bannatyne is a successful businessman because his risks are calculated.

Bannatyne also wants to see an outline of how the business will operate, reach its target customers, who'll be employed, how much of their own money a would-be entrepreneur is putting into the project and how he will be paid back. One thing that seems to annoy Bannatyne and the other Dragons is people who aren't putting their own money in. They feel that if you're not prepared to back your own idea, why should they? Investors usually want to invest for a short time, make money and get out. Bannatyne is no different, so he wants to know how you plan to buy him out of the business.

WHEN PLANS GO AWRY – WHY BUSINESSES FAIL

Many businesses don't make it as far as their first birthday and many more don't last beyond three years. But it's hard to tell if that's because they fail or because their owners feel they've done all they can with them and move on to another venture. But when a business does fail, it will be down to something the owner hasn't done well – and in Bannatyne's view, this will usually be research. Without research, he says, you won't know whether there's a big enough market for what your business has to offer, or how much money you'll need to get it up and running properly or prevent it running out of cash, or you'll end up with too much stock or not enough.

Apart from the lack of research, Bannatyne says, businesses fail because the owners employ too many staff instead of doing the work themselves or take too much money out of the business before it is mature enough to support them. Research, planning, hard work and putting money back into the business seem to be the way that Bannatyne makes his businesses sustainable.

PLAN YOUR ENTERPRISE

- **Know your customers.** Do an initial calculation as Bannatyne does, to work out how many customers you're likely to have, how much each will pay and what your costs will be. If the customers won't cover the costs, it's not going to be a viable business.
- **Bannatyne is prepared to accept that the business isn't viable and walk away.** It's better than spending a lot of money to have it fail later.
- **Work out what would happen if costs went up and customer numbers fell.** Bannatyne calculates how much change his business could cope with. It will give you an idea of how robust the business is likely to be and therefore how much risk you're taking with your investment.
- **If you think the business is viable, do a detailed plan.** Bannatyne says even if you don't need to borrow any money to get started, your plan will be a useful, detailed document of how you're going to run your operation and what your targets are. Don't forget to read it regularly and update it as circumstances change.
- **Be thorough as you write your business plan.** If you need to borrow money, make sure your plan is detailed and addresses all the questions an investor like Bannatyne will want answers to, including 'When will I get my money back?' and 'What will my return be?'

6

NEVER MIND THE ATRIUM!

'And, one suspects, you can either take him or leave him. He is who he is. And the same goes for his plain, head office.'[1]

– **Anonymous,** *Darlington and Stockton Times*

You can have the best business in the world: a great idea, the best possible research and a faultless business plan. But if you put it in the wrong place, it won't fly. That goes for web businesses as well as bricks and mortar businesses. If your potential customers, to whom you are targeting your service or product, can't get access to you easily, they'll give up trying and go elsewhere.

THE CREAM OF LOCATIONS

Duncan Bannatyne has always had an eye for a good location. From his first days of selling ice cream in Stockton-on-Tees, he's been well aware that there's only so far customers will go to buy your product. If the competition is in a better location, more convenient to customers, the customers will go there instead. Convenience can be as important as price and it's something the supermarkets have really understood.

The concession that Bannatyne bought as an ice cream seller, for example, gave him access to a very lucrative site in a local park without the competition being able to muscle in.

TOP OF THE PLOTS

The decision about where Bannatyne would build his first nursing home was made for him when he walked past an estate agent's window and saw a plot of land advertised. It already had planning permission for sheltered housing and when he checked with the local planning department, he discovered that a nursing home fell within the definition of sheltered housing.

The plot, in Darlington, was three quarters of an acre of derelict land. All around it was land next to the railway line that was being sold cheaply because the government wanted developers to build and make the view from the train more appealing. Despite the fact that Bannatyne's plot didn't fall into that category, and wasn't subsidized, he recognized that where developers built houses there would be a need for a nursing home. He has that kind of mind; always seeing what's out there and being able to work out how it could fit in with his business plans.

Convenience can be as important as price and it's something the supermarkets have really understood.

Even if he hadn't built on the plot, the land would have increased in value just because it was next to land that was being developed. He couldn't lose, but the banks refused to lend him the money unless he put his house up as security.

That was the first of his chain of Quality Care Homes. It was the beginning of his personal training in property development and was to stand Bannatyne in good stead over the years. Dealing with the banks, architects and builders honed his negotiating skills. He had to sell just about everything he owned, including the ice cream business, to get the home launched – but it was to be the first of many. These are the kinds of risks that put other people off running with their business ideas but which Bannatyne seems to relish and have little fear of. With each new home he improved the facilities and learned from his mistakes: 'We didn't build beautiful buildings; we built buildings around the needs of our residents.'[2]

A PLOT OF GOLD

His next plot was almost as uninspiring as the first. He was driving home and saw a 'For Sale' sign. Upon inspection he found another derelict patch of ground near a factory. He did his back-of-a-fag-packet calculation and worked out that if he bought the plot, there would be room for three nursing homes and he could keep his costs down. That seems to have been the moment when the pound signs floated in front of Bannatyne's eyes and he started to think in terms of millions.

The factory next door to the new plot was closing down and because the council was keen to announce new jobs coming to the area, it processed Bannatyne's planning application quickly. He employed the same architect and builder who'd worked on his first nursing home because they'd done a good job and their knowledge of the project meant the job would be done quickly.

He has that kind of mind; always seeing what's out there and being able to work out how it could fit in with his business plans.

From there, the Quality Care Homes business expanded rapidly. By the end of 1991 he had nine homes. He was using company profits to fund expansion and taking a very modest salary. Although on paper Bannatyne was fairly wealthy by this time, he wasn't leading a successful entrepreneur's lifestyle. He ploughed money back into his businesses and paid the interest on his loans out of cash flow if at all possible.

It's another of the principles of business that Bannatyne seems to have followed consistently and understood innately: where other business people make the mistake of taking money out of their business too soon to fund a luxury lifestyle, even as far back as Duncan's Super Ices he was building his businesses on a firm financial footing before thinking about spending on himself. Quality Care Homes was beginning to attract the attention of other entrepreneurs and Bannatyne had a bid to buy the company. He rejected it as too low, but he started to think about floating on the stock market to pay off his debts and get his hands on some of the wealth that he'd accumulated.

He ploughed money back into his businesses and paid the interest on his loans out of cash flow if at all possible.

The flotation was followed in 1993 by a skiing accident. Bannatyne had been enjoying a bit of off-piste skiing when he hit another skier, landed awkwardly and snapped the ligaments around his knee. The accident led to Bannatyne having to retire to the gym to build up damaged leg muscles. Whilst spending time in there he decided that he could build himself a new business in the health and leisure sector.

When Bannatyne and his first wife Gail had difficulty finding nursery places for their two youngest daughters, he decided to build his own day care centre. They wanted them both to be in the same nursery and that proved to be impossible. So what do you do in that situation if you're an entrepreneur at a loose end? Build your own day care centre. While Bannatyne was still keen on the idea of building health clubs, the nurseries took priority. He asked the board of Quality Care Homes to start up a subsidiary nursery business and when they said no, he set up a new business and started again.

RIGHT TIME, RIGHT PLACE

When others see what's always been there, Bannatyne can see how something could be done differently. For example, when he came across a car showroom for sale, he saw a large site in the middle of a residential neighbourhood. He knew instinctively that the residents would prefer to have a facility that helped them rather than a car showroom. It's another of the attributes that's helped him to succeed.

Another thing he'd learned was to buy the premises subject to planning permission. If he didn't get to do what he wanted with the site, he could walk away without any money having changed hands. Despite a few hiccups, he eventually got planning permission to change the car showroom into a children's day care centre. He instructed an architect to design a building around the requirements of the legislation. The nursery was designed to cut down on the need for supervision, with toilets attached to each room, each room opening onto the playground, integrated kitchens and washrooms, and CCTV and alarm systems.

As soon as the first Just Learning day care centre was open, Bannatyne began to plan more. As well as building his own, Bannatyne bought out other day care centres, including a chain of nurseries in Kent where the seller had lost his licence and needed to sell quickly.

A HEALTHY REGARD FOR LOCATION

At last it was time to start up the health clubs that had been on Bannatyne's mind for several years. He bought a plot of land near

Stockton-on-Tees for a nursery but as soon as the deal was signed, he realized he'd bought twice as much land as he needed. Joanne McCue, Director of Nursing at Quality Care Homes, suggested he use the rest of the plot for the site of the long-anticipated health club.

When others see what's always been there, Bannatyne can see how something could be done differently.

The plot was in the middle of a huge housing development where there would be few other facilities – it was an ideal location. Building of the first Bannatyne Health and Leisure club started in 1997 and the team used all the knowledge of building that they'd accumulated from the care homes and the nurseries. Bannatyne realized that what he'd really become was a property developer.

Bannatyne knew there's no point in building a health club too far away from the people who'll want to use it. He knew that people were not prepared to drive for miles to do some exercise. The second club was in the middle of a big housing development and Bannatyne's first foray outside the north-east. The site was too big for the health centre, so Bannatyne and his team built a day care nursery on it too and left the rest of the plot vacant. The vacant plot was put to good use later and acted as a land bank – the money was in the land instead of the bank.

By 2001, the health clubs were working well and the team had worked out a set of criteria to help them decide where and when to open next. Bannatyne sold Just Learning in 2001 for £22 million to the investment company Alchemy Partners.

In the next three years, another 23 health clubs opened. Bannatyne looks for an area that doesn't already have a health club and then works out how many people live within a ten-minute drive of where he wants to build. From there he researches how many of those could afford his membership fees before he decides whether to go ahead. If the figures don't add up, he walks away.

SPACED OUT

As the club chain grew, so too did the number of specialist suppliers Bannatyne met. Because he was putting so much work their way he could negotiate better deals. But he also realized that a lot of the space in his buildings wasn't used efficiently. There were corridors and staircases that didn't make money. When Tony Bell investigated he found that a little over a quarter of the space wasn't used and so they worked with the architects to cut down on wasted space like stairwells and corridors, and create more efficient ways of using space. For example, by combining the reception and lounge areas, the same staff could serve coffees and check people in – so saving on the wage bill as well as the building costs.

MOVING ON

While he was building up Bannatyne Fitness and juggling it with Just Learning, Bannatyne's enterprises were run from home. In the late 1990s he had to find office space and bought some premises around the corner from his house.

By 2003, the office was too small. Bannatyne got planning permission for the building to be knocked down and flats to be built on the site. He sold the office with the planning permission at a massive profit – his first profit as a property developer – and bought the Old Power House in Darlington, the former headquarters of the electricity board. The transaction made Bannatyne think of a future in residential property and turned to the unused part of his plot in Essex that had been 'land banked'. He got planning permission to build homes on it and Bannatyne Housing was born.

The Old Power House became Bannatyne's new headquarters. He's never remodelled the building, which is too big for his needs. It doesn't have impressive entrances or mezzanine floors. Much of it is empty but he doesn't see the point in having glamorous offices when he can be making profits instead.

NEVER MIND THE ATRIUM!

- **Get out there and look for the right location for your business.** Bannatyne often spots them while walking or driving past. Just because a site is used as one thing doesn't mean it wouldn't be better suited to a different kind of business. Your own locality can be a good place to start, as you'll know a lot about the area and the potential customers.
- **Work out how far customers are likely to travel to buy what you have to sell.** Then work out whether or not there are enough of them within that distance who can afford what you plan to offer. Bannatyne's ten minute driving test!
- **Build your premises around the needs of the people who'll use them** as Bannatyne does, and build them to meet the legal requirements right from the start.
- **Use as much of the building as possible in ways that bring you income.** Empty space uses heat and gives you no return as Bannatyne discovered.
- **Look for ways to integrate working areas** so that you can cut down on staff and wages bills. Bannatyne does it with his hotels and fitness centres.
- **Don't let your ego run away with you.** Bannatyne doesn't need impressive mezzanine floors and an atrium. Keep your overheads low with modest premises.
- **Get to know your suppliers, architects and builders, and do deals as Bannaytne does.** If they know you'll hire them again and again, they're more likely to do the job for fixed rates. And they'll come up with more cost-effective building practices and get quicker with each project they work on.

7

HAVE THE RIGHT PEOPLE BY YOUR SIDE

'Bannatyne's unfaltering self-assurance could be mistaken for arrogance, except for the Dragon's habit of praising others with equal gusto.'[1]

– Rebecca Burn-Callander, realbusiness.co.uk

At each stage of business, Bannatyne says he's looked for ways to add value for the customer: en suite bathrooms in his care homes, convenient facilities for the children and staff of the nurseries, and better quality than that provided by his competitors. Everything he's said and written confirms his commitment to pleasing his customers to keep them coming back, offering them new products and services so that they buy more from his businesses.

But he also says over and over again that he'd have got nowhere if he hadn't had the right staff – people he could delegate to while he got on with running and expanding his businesses. Bannatyne suggests he is not a good people person and is not a natural at managing people, yet he believes in looking after his staff. Many have felt loved and stayed with him for years, but not all of those who've worked for him would agree that they were looked after. As in any business, on occasions he has sacked staff or made changes that employees disliked and so they resigned. But he does pay bonuses to staff for meeting their target sales. On *Dragons' Den* he can come across as the harsh Dragon who doesn't suffer fools, but in his own business he believes in supporting and training staff to help them reach their potential and progress through the organization.

He believes you have to make staff *want* to work for you.

He believes you have to make staff *want* to work for you. And then there's delegation to those loyal employees. By allowing them to get on with their jobs, and make and learn from their mistakes, Bannatyne can trust them and delegate further – eventually, he only has to come in for five hours a week and can spend the rest of the time growing the business, looking for the next business opportunity or even lying by the pool at his luxury villa in Cannes. People, he says, are the key to a successful business. It's hardly a new business concept, but it's one that many entrepreneurs fail to grasp – to the detriment of their enterprises.

LEARNING THE HARD WAY

Bannatyne's first attempts at employing staff taught him a lesson. He was expanding his ice cream empire and it wasn't hard to identify the skills required to put more vans on the road. He didn't really need people with complementary skills: he needed people like him who could drive, and sell ice cream. All went well for a while. He drove most of his vans to their sites in parks, employed people to sell, collected the vans in the evening and did the ordering, stock taking, admin and figures himself.

What didn't work so well was entrusting the business to someone else while he took time off. This became apparent when his wife Gail needed urgent eye surgery to save her sight. Bannatyne left the business in what he thought were the capable hands of his most honest driver. The eye surgery was a success but by the time he got back to work, the business had gone down the pan.

Bannatyne went back to his old way of working and eventually rebuilt the business. He liked the admin side of running it and went direct to the relevant government departments to find out about his responsibilities as an employer and about VAT, National Insurance and tax. Long days of hard work built up an annual turnover of £300,000, with about £60,000 of profit – not bad in 1979. But you can't build a business empire if you have to do all the jobs yourself.

A JOINT VENTURE

When Bannatyne opened a residential home in Scarborough with his neighbour, it was the first time he had worked with a business partner. However, it did not work out too well after his partner contracted the builders and agreed to pay them by the day, which almost led to bankruptcy.

On top of that, Bannatyne seems to have realized that he doesn't like handing over control, something he experienced again later on when he was floating his company on the Stock Exchange and had to have other people on board. He advocates delegation, but handing over control is a whole different ball game.

ON HIS OWN AGAIN

The residential home was launched successfully, but when Bannatyne wanted to go from there into nursing homes, he decided to go it alone. His first home had single rooms, the majority of which had their own toilets. It was a new kind of nursing home at that time, and a new kind of business for Bannatyne.

As many successful entrepreneurs like Bannatyne suggest, you can get experience and confidence by being in business, even if it doesn't all work out as you hoped. Whatever business he was in, Bannatyne seems to have been driven by the desire and commitment to be the best. The nursing homes were a new venture but he took to it the lessons of his past enterprises. His former business partner had also decided to go into nursing homes and having a rival spurred Bannatyne on to do things better.

GETTING THE STAFF

In the ice cream business, all the jobs were ones that Bannatyne could do. In the nursing home business, Bannatyne needed qualified, specialist staff – people he could trust to get on with their jobs and do them well. His first appointment was his manager.

He advertised and employed Margaret, who worked for a rival care home company. She was impressed with his plan for every resident to have their own room and bathroom. Margaret brought with her a lot of experience and all the information Bannatyne needed about rules and regulations. She was a very experienced nurse and handled the red tape and hiring the other staff. It can be difficult to find qualified staff in a sector that's growing, so poaching staff from other companies can sometimes be the only way to get them apart from training them yourself. That can mean having to give someone an incentive to leave their current employer. Bannatyne seems to have realized early on that money isn't the only incentive and that bonuses, working conditions and working for a firm that believes in doing things better can be more of an incentive.

He advocates delegation, but handing over control is a whole different ball game.

But not all the staff were perfect. Many of the nursing homes were in deprived areas and many residents paid cash from their pensions, so the inevitable happened. Upon investigation, it became clear to Bannatyne that one particular member of staff was to blame for some money going missing. He confronted her, she confessed and was given a second chance. However, when the same nurse took money a second time, she was dismissed. Incidents like this were the exception rather than the rule, but it shows that he was prepared to listen to reason and try to help staff through difficult times.

DELEGATION

It's when it comes to staff that Bannatyne claims to have learned the most important lesson. Time and again in interviews, he says he's convinced that his success lies in employing the right staff for the job and letting them do that job. He claims that he's always found delegation natural – just common sense. It frees him up to run his businesses more dynamically, with time to see the bigger picture and work out the next moves.

He points out that if he had spent time on the details, he wouldn't have had the time to look for new sites for his care homes, to study what his competition was up to, or to negotiate new contracts. He admits that it's easier delegating to good people who know how to take care of the details, so the key is to build the right team.

Delegation to staff he can trust may well be the reason his career has been so successful, and also why he's been able to spend more time with his family and ultimately on his charity work, TV shows and books. But delegation works two ways because it allows staff to develop and find out about their own strengths. That's very motivating for people and breeds loyalty, and may be one of the main reasons so many of the Bannatyne staff have stayed with him for so long.

Bannatyne seems to have realized early on that money isn't the only incentive.

He tells people who go to listen to him speak that they shouldn't worry about the legal responsibilities that go with growing a big business, because if you learn to delegate and to pick the right people, and build the right team, you can employ people to handle the complexities of big business for you. As he's become more experienced and grown more successful, he seems to have become more convinced that delegation is the key.

TEAM-BUILDING

Bannatyne claims to follow his instincts rather than rely on CVs to tell the truth about a candidate. He seems to feel the best candidates may not have the best CVs. It's possible that because he didn't have a particularly inspiring CV himself in the early years, he understands that qualifications aren't always the most important proof of a person's ability to do a particular job.

Bannatyne learned a lot about the failings of CVs when he took part in *Break with the Boss*, a TV series from 2006. Three of his employees got the pleasure of going on holiday with their boss for three days and at the end of the trip he was to decide which one should be promoted.

Over the three days, Bannatyne realized that the standard method of recruitment – a CV and a relatively short interview – leaves a lot to be desired. His opinion of his three employees changed over the break and he resolved to spend more time in future when he appoints senior directors.

What he seems to value most is loyalty. As an example, he cites the candidate he hired who'd been with her previous employer for 12 years before she was made redundant. She worked for Bannatyne for 20 years and was a key member of his team until she retired in 2006. And he showed his appreciation of another loyal member of staff when she was bereaved, paying her until she was well enough to return to work.

Bannatyne also seems to understand the value of training for all concerned. When he opened his first day care centre, half of the staff had to have a recognized childcare qualification. The staff weren't available to hire, so he realized the best way was to train them through the company. The employees were all encouraged to work towards NVQs.

What he seems to value most is loyalty.

It was a similar story when he set up his first health clubs. The supply of qualified gym staff was limited, so he trained his own. He started his own courses and every employee was invited to apply for training that would lead to promotion. Bannatyne discovered that it's not just beneficial for the staff, but it's a relatively inexpensive way to keep them and motivate them – and because of that, the costs of recruiting go down. What's good for staff is usually good for customers and therefore good for the business.

He also seems to understand the value of supporting new staff. He recognizes that if someone isn't meeting their targets it might be because they're not getting the support they need, or their job is too much for one person, rather than a sign that they're not up to the job.

GETTING THE BEST OUT OF PEOPLE

Bannatyne believes in rewarding people for a job well done. He implements bonus schemes that are related to targets. For example, when his nursing homes were 98% full, everyone on the team got an annual bonus – including the cleaning staff.

Bannatyne believes that everyone should share in the success of the business. He rewards his employees with bonuses and offers share option schemes to his directors. Bannatyne believes in making everyone part of the team. He's loyal to them and they're loyal to him.

RIGHT PERSON, RIGHT TIME

One of Bannatyne's contractors estimated that Bannatyne owed him £50,000. Bannatyne estimated the figure to be around £10,000, but was willing to go to £20,000. While the debate was raging, Bannatyne received a CV from Tony Bell, who at the time was a project manager and experienced quantity surveyor, with experience in conflict resolution. Bannatyne asked Tony to resolve the dispute with the contractor but refused to pay him.

Bell agreed to do the job on the basis that if he got the contractor to settle for anything less than £20,000, he would take a quarter of the saving as his fee. The contractor settled for £15,000 – saving Bannatyne £5000, of which Tony took £1250. Bannatyne didn't have a job to give him but as soon as he could, he employed Bell as Director of Projects, helping to build up and manage Bannatyne Fitness.

He extends the philosophy to people he buys services from too, such as builders and architects. If they can use faster methods and cheaper suppliers, and so make savings, Bannatyne shares those savings with them.

For the same reason, Bannatyne doesn't seem to be in favour of outsourcing, arguing that if you contract out services, such as cleaning, you get different people doing the job so they don't get to know the business and the staff. They aren't part of the team, so team spirit breaks down. They never feel that they have a stake in the company. The most successful members of Bannatyne's staff are those he's nurtured himself.

However, it's not all share options and bonuses working for Bannatyne. Employees are paid slightly above the industry average to attract the best, but they're paid the statutory levels of maternity, paternity and sick pay. The get generous amounts of leave for bereavement, for instance, but they don't get away with running up big personal phone bills or spending all day surfing the net. Employees have to bring their bills, with business calls highlighted, to be reimbursed. Bannatyne says it's not about the money – it's about the principle.

He also employs mystery shoppers in his health clubs. They pretend to be potential members and wear hidden cameras. Staff are told when they join that they'll never know when their dealing with a mystery shopper. It's not only a way of checking on how clean and well run a club is, but Bannatyne can see how individual employees perform and talent-spot people who might be right for promotion.

TEAM BANNATYNE

Chris Rutter was Bannatyne's financial director for Quality Care Homes. He was a very hard worker who got on with the job, was accurate and could work complicated projections out quickly. He got the job when a highly recommended financial director from a big firm of accountants, with a tremendous track record, couldn't settle into working for a firm where he didn't have a department at his beck and call. Chris stayed with Quality Care Homes after Bannatyne sold it in 1997.

Joanne McCue joined Quality Care Homes as a nursing sister and after a few years took over as Director of Nursing. After his first marriage broke down, Joanne moved in with her boss and they had two children.

OTHER IMPORTANT PEOPLE IN BANNATYNE'S LIFE

Although he didn't want the same things, Bannatyne always respected his father and was upset when his father said of his first business venture 'people like us don't run businesses'. When his father told him he was proud of his achievements after the opening of the first care home, that spurred Bannatyne on to follow up that achievement with others he could be proud of.

In 1996, John Moreton led a bid by US company Southern Cross to take over Quality Care Homes. Bannatyne and the board rejected the offer, but Moreton impressed him and they became very close friends. Moreton was very moved by what Bannatyne told him about his charity work in Romania and now funds several projects there too.

Nigel Armstrong was an accountant who could sketch out a business model in a few minutes and contacted Bannatyne for work soon after the sale of Quality Care Homes. He got the job that Chris Rutter had vacated. From Financial Controller, Nigel became Managing Director, and – according to Bannatyne in his book *Anyone Can Do It* – has share options worth millions of pounds.

MENTORS

Bannatyne advocates in interviews that business people find themselves mentors, who can be worth their weight in gold. Be they family members, friends, investors or other entrepreneurs, it's good to have people who listen to your business woes and offer a different perspective. The ideal mentor would be someone who has the right skills for your business and can pass on their own knowledge and experience – just talking a problem through with someone is often enough to help you see the wood for the trees.

Bannatyne believes that everyone should share in the success of the business.

Bannatyne suggests that details of mentors be included in your business plan as they can help sway investors in your favour and that they can help with recruitment and interviewing, be at meetings while you're growing the business, and challenge your assumptions. A really good mentor will probably have useful contacts you can use too. If you feel uneasy about taking up someone's time and bending their ear about your business problems, offer them a small stake in the business.

CONTACTS AND NETWORKING

When he'd been in the north-east of England for a while, Bannatyne thought that a few more contacts might be good for business. He joined the local pay-and-play golf course. Ice cream salespeople work mostly evenings and weekends – when other people play golf. So on invitation he joined the Freemasons, hoping it would be good for business. But he soon realized that networking wasn't for him.

Despite that, he advises that the world is full of people who can help you and you'll meet them at trade fairs, exhibitions, the local chamber of commerce and online on sites like LinkedIn and Facebook: 'I know some people whose single most important skill as an entrepreneur is their ability to network'. [2] His tip is to research the work of someone whose help you'd like, so if you do meet them at an industry event, you'll have something to talk to them about and they'll be impressed by how much you know about them. If you're going to a seminar, for example, try to get a delegate list beforehand and do your research.

HAVE THE RIGHT PEOPLE BY YOUR SIDE

- **Get staff who want to work for you.** Bannatyne's people work hard and are committed and loyal. He prizes loyalty very highly and believes in paying bonuses for a job well done. But he understands that money isn't the only incentive and that training and responsibility create loyalty in staff too.
- **Not all skills will be on a CV.** Bannatyne doesn't always select his people on the basis of their application; sometimes people bring other skills that aren't on the job description but are just as valuable. He listens to his gut instinct and it has proved to be a useful recruitment tool.
- **Encourage staff to find their strengths.** The people Bannatyne hires may not be the best managers when they first get the job, but they're capable of finding their strengths and building their departments around them in the way he's built his businesses around his strengths.
- **Delegation is easy if you've got the right people.** Bannatyne looks for trustworthy people who he can delegate to and can be left to get on with their jobs.
- **Having a skilled, motivated team will let you develop the business.** Bannatyne wants people who are good at their jobs, motivated, and as passionate about the business as he is. He wants to delegate to them and their complementary skills, so he can get on with running his business more dynamically and enjoying life.

8

MAKE MONEY, EXPAND RAPIDLY, THEN MAKE MORE MONEY

'[Duncan Bannatyne] intends to give away 95% of his wealth before he dies, which he hopes will be at least 40 years hence.'[1]

– **Paul Dalgrano,** *Sunday Herald*

He may have been a late entrepreneurial starter, but once he got the bit between his teeth there was no stopping Duncan Bannatyne building a successful business empire. When he came to *Dragons' Den*, and to wider public attention, he was worth £130 million. The latest estimate of his wealth is £320 million.

The word most often used about Bannatyne on *Dragons' Den* is 'canny', a Scottish word that means thrifty – prudent rather than mean, someone who can save the pennies and watch the pounds pile up in the bank.

A POOR BEGINNING

Bannatyne's story is a real rags-to-riches tale. His siblings dispute his version of their upbringing to a certain extent. The disparity in family recall may be down to perception and expectation, or to Duncan being the second eldest. By the time his youngest brother Sandy was born, Duncan was already in the Navy. The family may not have been so hard up by the time the younger children came along.

Whatever the detail, Bannatyne remembers being poor and wanting to have a different life. That memory seems to underpin his drive and, combined with the determination he says he inherited from his father, has fermented a lasting ambition to make money. Bannatyne never apologizes for making money or for always wanting to make more. Even now, when he has more than he can ever spend, he still refuses to sit back and enjoy retirement. He is still driven to seek out the next opportunity and create a successful business from it. Perhaps the truth is that when you have that kind of entrepreneurial mind, with its natural restlessness, you simply can't sit back and retire.

He has made money from ice cream, care homes, children's nurseries, health clubs, hotels, spas, residential property and investing in and running other people's companies, as well as being a Business Angel. He really does merit the title 'serial entrepreneur'.

OLDER, WISER AND WEALTHIER

Bannatyne has accumulated wealth of around £320 million at 60 years old, from a standing start at 30. He is never one to miss a business opportunity and claims he's never had an original business idea in his life, but has made his money improving on other people's products and services.

The template for making his businesses successful seems to be borrowing, paying back the interest on the debt out of cash flow if possible while taking only a modest salary, ploughing any profit back into the business, expanding quickly and not being afraid of taking on more debt.

BE THE BEST, NOT THE CHEAPEST

Bannatyne's first business was financed from his own earnings at a bakery in Stockton-on-Tees. He worked the unpopular night shift and supplemented that income by buying cars at auction to repair and sell on. It was there that he bought his first ice cream van to start up Duncan's Super Ices.

He kept costs down by buying from the cheapest ice cream supplier he could find and sold at higher prices than rivals because he added value to his products – with names and faces on the ice creams that the children loved. He was determined to be the best ice cream seller in the north-east, not the cheapest. 'Be the best, not the cheapest' is a business philosophy he carried through into all his subsequent business ventures.

THE FIRST OF MANY

Quality Care Homes evolved from one co-owned residential home in Scarborough into a chain of homes around the north-east. Bannatyne – perhaps naively – thought that because he had six ice cream vans with an annual turnover of £300,000 and a profit of around £60,000, several terraced houses let out to tenants and a profitable residential care home already up and running, the banks would fall over themselves to lend him the money he needed to build his first nursing home. And who could blame him? He would seem to have just the right profile for a bank keen to invest. But it wasn't that simple.

He really does merit the title 'serial entrepreneur'.

Margaret Thatcher had just brought in the Registered Homes Act 1984 to pay for older people in care. Bannatyne calculated that if he built a 50-room care home, he'd have a guaranteed income of £364,000 a year paid by the government. He worked out his likely costs and that if the home was constantly 90% full, he could make a 33% profit on his investment every year. How could the bank manager fail to be impressed by the figures? But the bank manager declined his offer to invest.

Bannatyne had to put up his home as security for a loan that he used to buy the land to build his nursing home on. The home had to be built before the bank would lend him any money against the property. Undeterred, he found an architect and builder and funded the project himself. And that's when he came up with his next money mantra, another one he's taken with him through his business career: 'never pay by the day'.

Already in debt for the land, anything and everything he owned had to be sold to pay for the building. Eventually the terraced houses and the ice cream business went too, and he borrowed the maximum on each of his three credit cards. In the end he had no choice but to do a deal whereby the builder would wait until the project was finished before he got the remainder of his money. The builder elicited a high interest rate on that outstanding money.

Bannatyne has described the decision to float, and the whole floatation process, as swimming in shark-infested waters.

Perhaps the experience is the reason why Bannatyne doesn't seem to have much patience with would-be business people who don't use their own capital or the value of their homes to finance their businesses. If they really believed in themselves and their ventures, they'd be willing to risk their own money. If they aren't willing to take that risk then why should he?

When the first nursing home was built and fully occupied, Bannatyne got his money. The bank valued his business at £600,000 and lent him 70% of that. The project including land, building costs, professional fees and equipping and furnishing the home had cost him £360,000. With the money from the bank he paid the builder and the credit cards, and immediately started to expand the home.

Bannatyne had money in the bank and a guaranteed income from nursing home fees. He looked around for his next site and the next. Because it was the late 1980s and interest rates were going up, Bannatyne negotiated a 'cap and collar' deal on his bank loans. If rates continued going up, there was a ceiling beyond which his rates wouldn't rise, and if they fell again his rates would only come down so far. If interest rates fell dramatically he could end up paying over the odds, but it gave him some peace of mind to know what his maximum payments would be.

DEEPER AND DEEPER IN DEBT

The more Bannatyne borrowed, the slower the process got. Initially the local bank manager could approve his loans but as he wanted to borrow more, the manager's boss had to be consulted – and then the boss's boss. Bannatyne then shopped around for better deals at other banks. Eventually he was able to start building new homes without waiting for loans to be approved. His lenders got cold feet and worried he might have bitten off more than he could chew. They couldn't verify his total debts or assets, and thought he was expanding too quickly. His loans dried up. He had to stop work on two homes and leave them unfinished until he could finish them using the profits from existing operating homes.

By 1991, Bannatyne had nine homes with 428 beds and debts of £6 million. He wanted to build more, but the banks refused to lend and he started thinking about selling. He could sell a couple of homes and use the money to build more or sell the whole business. One offer would have given him £6 million to spend but when he checked out the share prices of similar care homes businesses listed on the Stock Exchange he realized that Quality Cares Homes business was worth more. The third option was to float.

FLOATING – JUST!

In interviews Bannatyne has described the decision to float, and the whole floatation process, as swimming in shark-infested waters. Part of the problem was that he knew nothing about stock market floatation. He had to learn from books and through trial and error. He discovered that City investors would pay him for a share of his business. He imagined he'd have the cash to spend on his expansion ambitions and still run his own show, and that appealed.

Delegation comes naturally to him and is the commonsense way to run a business.

Bannatyne learned the floatation jargon and found a broker prepared to take him on. He then discovered that he was losing control of his own firm. He realized that the broker's recommendations about how to change the company to make it attractive to investors were really instructions rather then helpful suggestions, and he didn't like having to answer to someone else. Nor did he like the fact that all the lawyers, brokers and bankers he had to deal with were making a profit at his expense.

One major change to the business was to set up a board of non-executive directors: people who represent the interests of the shareholders, professional people with useful experience to bring to the table. Bannatyne feels these are just 'jobs of the boys'. His newly appointed chairman was paid £20,000 a year and had a share option for two days' work a month. It wasn't a situation Bannatyne felt comfortable with but it was a means to an end.

USUAL PRACTICE

Worse was to come, though. Bannatyne was very aggrieved to discover that on top of the brokers' fee of £80,000 and the salaries of the board, he had to pay a PR company to sell the company to potential investors. It was when he got their first bill that he encountered 'usual practice'. The PR company's expenses added just over a fifth to its bill and there was nothing in the contract about expenses. Bannatyne argued, but without the PR firm he couldn't float.

There was also a battle with the broker over the share price. The broker wanted to keep the share price down to attract investment. Bannatyne wanted to keep it high so that he'd have to sell fewer shares in his company to bring in the cash he needed. The broker wanted to raise £20 million but Bannatyne didn't want to go from owning almost all of his business to owning a minority stake in it. He wanted to raise enough to clear his £6 million debt and pay for the next round of expansion. In the end they agreed to sell off 27%, leaving Bannatyne with 72.8% and still in charge.

Bannatyne was determined to expand as quickly as possible.

The whole process took about six months and was almost called off at the last minute because Bannatyne realized that the brokers' fee of £80,000 had – because of 'usual practice' – swollen to £92,500. He refused to pay and the broker threatened to stop the floatation. In the end, Bannatyne's Chairman rode to the rescue, calmed everyone down and the floatation went ahead – but Bannatyne didn't pay the brokers' expenses. The deal earned Bannatyne a reputation for being a hard operator and he was applauded by other business people as the person who'd taken on the City and won. He walked away with half a million in his personal account and £4 million in the company account

ANSWERING TO THE BOARD

Bannatyne enjoyed running Quality Care Homes, despite having the board and shareholders to answer to and the company carried on expanding rapidly. The Chief Executive and the board did argue though over how to finance the expansion. Bannatyne wanted to go on borrowing rather than selling more shares and wanted to keep his 72% stake. The board took the opposite view. In 1994 he did raise more money through selling more shares, bringing his own shareholding down to 50.8%, but for a different reason.

The floatation had been stressful for Bannatyne but it also heralded the beginning of the end of his first marriage. Gail had been a bit shocked to discover that her husband had used their home as security to buy the plot for his first nursing home – according to *Anyone Can Do It*, she said 'You spent £30,000 of our money on that. Are you out of your mind?' – but she had supported him all the way. But she seemed less comfortable with the floatation. He was unhappy. They were growing apart. Despite the fact that she was pregnant with their fourth child, they agreed at a trial separation. This was followed in 1994 by divorce.

Bannatyne sold shares in Quality Care Homes to give Gail a divorce settlement worth £6 million. That amounted to about half of his wealth at the time and brought his shareholding down to 50.8%, but he was absolutely convinced he was on track to make a whole lot more.

Two years after the floatation, Bannatyne took over as Chairman as well as Chief Executive because, despite being warned that the move would cause the company's share price to drop temporarily, he wanted to be fully in control again. Delegation comes naturally to him and is the commonsense way to run a business, but not being in control is different and not something Bannatyne feels comfortable with.

But even regaining control wasn't enough. His restlessness got the better of him again and he was ready to move on to something new. He launched Just Learning and opened the first day care nursery at the end of 1996, started building the first Bannatyne Health and Leisure Centre in 1997, and sold his remaining shares in Quality Care Homes that summer.

PASTURES NEW

By the time he launched Bannatyne Health and Leisure (later Bannatyne Fitness) he had brought Tony Bell on board. Bell was an experienced quantity surveyor and project manager and helped Bannatyne deal with the contractors. He set up a scheme whereby if the builders managed to find a way to reduce building costs by doing something in a more cost-effective way, the savings were split between the company and the builder.

The team nurturing the new business was Bannatyne, Joanne McCue (who was living with Bannatyne by then) and Tony Bell.

Bannatyne relished getting back to running his businesses without having to answer to a board and shareholders. He had money in the bank and there was no one in a planning department holding up his progress.

RAPID EXPANSION

Bannatyne invested £16 million in four fitness clubs but, as with Quality Care Homes, it wasn't enough. It wasn't growing fast enough. He repeated his pattern of buying land and starting to build before he had the money in place to finish the clubs. At one stage he had seven clubs at various stages of construction. He had appointed Nigel Armstrong as his new Financial Director. His original Financial Director Chris Rutter stayed with Quality Cares Homes when Bannatyne sold out. Armstrong was instructed only to pay people who screamed for their money. It was a baptism of fire.

Most Angel investors will want to invest in sectors that interest them, in their own local area, and will have their own lending criteria.

Bannatyne was determined to expand as quickly as possible. He was expanding so rapidly he was forced to move the office out of his house. He promoted Nigel Armstrong to Managing Director. He had clubs springing up all over the country and it was impossible for him and Nigel to keep a firm hand on the management of them all, so he appointed regional managers. Some of those were hired from outside but some were existing employees who were ready for a challenge and promotion.

Bannatyne had worked out that it was costing around £4 million to build a club to his standards and his target was a profit of £1 million a year from each club. That's a 25% return on his investment – the figure he tries to reach on *Dragons' Den* too. In 2001 Just Learning was sold, which freed up money for the expansion of Bannatyne Fitness – by 2004, they had built 23 clubs.

In 2004 they opened three more and in 2005 they opened just two. There were still towns without clubs, but the market was drying up. The only way to go on expanding was to buy up the opposition. In August 2006, Bannatyne Fitness almost doubled the size of its empire by taking over 24 health clubs from the Hilton Hotel group for £92 million.

OPPORTUNITIES ELSEWHERE

As well as his own business ventures, since 1996 Bannatyne has been using his expertise to help turn around other businesses investing in them at the same time. That experience stood him in good stead and made him a suitable panellist for *Dragons' Den*.

Dragons' Den is all about successful entrepreneurs investing in the businesses of other would-be entrepreneurs; investing their own money and using their expertise to help the business succeed and grow; and making a reasonable return for the Dragons along the way. But Duncan Bannatyne had become an Angel long before he became a Dragon.

DRAGON OR ANGEL?

Before the producers of *Dragons' Den* approached Bannatyne, he'd already dabbled as an investor in other businesses. The first ven-

HELP FROM THE GOVERNMENT

Bannatyne isn't a man to complain about government red tape. He's often benefited financially from government legislation.

During his ice cream days he also converted houses to bedsits when the government decided to pay rent directly to landlords who took in out-of-work tenants. He set up his nursing homes when the Government announced in 1984 that it would pay at least £140 a week for each elderly resident in care. And he sold Just Learning in 2001 for £22 million, even though he thought it was an inflated price.

Government regulations had played into his hands. In 1997 the investment regulations for all venture capital trusts (one of which was Alchemy, which bought Just Learning) had changed. Alchemy had to reinvest 70% of its money in qualifying industries such as the care industry. Having failed to buy Rover, the funds had to be reinvested within a certain period of time otherwise the backers would lose their tax breaks and wouldn't be eligible for 40% capital gains tax relief and 2% income tax relief.

ture he got involved in was New Life Care Services, which offered accommodation to people with learning difficulties and helped them to live independently. He was asked to become involved and took a 10% stake in the company for an investment of £40,000, becoming the company's chairman.

ANGEL INVESTORS

Business Angels (BAs) are wealthy individuals who invest in high-growth businesses in return for equity – a share of ownership – in those businesses. Some invest individually and others invest as part of a network, syndicate or investment club. They want to add to their own business portfolios and to their skill set. As well as money, BAs usually make their own skills, experience and contacts available to the company. It's often those additional assets that business people are looking for as they're the key to making a business grow quickly and succeed.

BAs may well step in where the banks are afraid to tread, often with smaller sums of money than banks are willing to commit. Somewhere between £10,000 and £750,000 is normal, and BAs are usually happy to take a bit of a risk. Most Angel investors will want to invest in sectors that interest them, in their own local area, and will have their own lending criteria. So what makes sense to one investor, because it's something they have experience of, won't necessarily appeal to another. Because they're on their home turf in terms of location and experience, BAs often make investment decisions quickly.

BAs are in the investment business to make money. That means they'll want to know when they'll get their money out, as well as what level of return they're likely to make. By being BAs they get the opportunity to be involved in the running of businesses they might otherwise not have thought of, and they often do it to learn something about businesses closely related to their own. Having a BA on board isn't for everyone, as they do tend to want quite a say in the way the company is run.

It had been set up by four men who all worked in the care profession but who had no experience of running a business. They didn't want to expand. Bannatyne wasn't happy at the lack of expansion and he was taking a salary and a healthy dividend for doing very little. In the end he advised the men to buy him and their other investors out. He wrote them a business plan and arranged a loan that allowed them to make monthly payments of less than they were paying all their investors. He walked away with £230,000.

Bannatyne's worth is estimated to have risen by about £10 million in the last year.

It may have been an exasperating experience over about two years, but it still gave Bannatyne a very healthy return on his original investment on top of the salary and dividends.

RADIO GA-GA

At the end of the 1990s the government was selling off radio frequencies to the highest bidders and a lot of investors were getting in on the act.

It was something completely different for Bannatyne. He was asked to be part of a consortium bidding for a frequency in the north-east of England. It wasn't successful, but it whetted his appetite to try his hand at something outside his usual sphere of expertise.

Later, when the chance came along to run the station for a friend who had won the frequency bid, he bought some shares and took a seat on the board. He has described what he found as the worst radio station in the world with next to no listeners. Less than three years after his first board meeting, Bannatyne had turned the station around and sold his shares for twice what he'd paid for them.

TAKING YOUR EYE OFF THE BALL

But not all his Business Angel ventures were a success. Lady in Leisure, the small women-only gym chain, lost Bannatyne more than £1 million. Only after he invested in the business, which he hoped to buy, did he realize how badly it was run. He quit and the firm went bust taking his investment with it.

From these experiences as an Angel Bannatyne knew, before *Dragons' Den* was ever commissioned, that an investor has to work with people with similar ambitions, must do extensive research into any business he or she intends to invest in, and can work their magic in companies that are outside their usual sector and are someone else's rather than their own.

PENNY-PINCHER OR CANNY OPERATOR?

Part of Bannatyne's business philosophy, which he has reiterated in many interviews and in his books, is 'don't spend money you don't need to spend'. Despite his bonuses and share options schemes for staff, 'generous' is not a word all of them use about their boss. He managed to get a reputation for being 'tight'. He puts this down to paperclips, pens and the incident of the boiled eggs.

He maintains there's no need for any organization to buy paperclips as they arrive every morning in the post. He has it written into staff contracts that they must provide their own pens after discovering that one of his nursing homes was getting through 200 a month. He is convinced that that's not mean or penny-pinching; it simply makes good business sense. He stopped short of calling in Inspector Poirot but even he admits that the investigation he launched into the fate of two hard-boiled eggs, which were in the kitchen after lunch but had later gone missing, was a step too far! It went on for weeks until he forgot about it.

The incident that really threatened to undermine his assertion that he's not 'tight' was that of the Kellogg's Cereal bars. Meant as a free promotion, the bars were given to Bannatyne Fitness but were sold to club members. One of the firm's employees exposed the 'rip-off' to the *Daily Mirror* and one of its reporters was charged 60 pence for three bars.

Another disgruntled employee told the *Daily Mirror* 'rather than learn from the error of its ways, the company launched a witch-hunt to find a scapegoat'. Kellogg's accused the firm of breach of contract, Bannatyne claimed that he knew nothing about a contract and that giving the bars away would have amounted to commercial suicide, further arguing that giving away bars in your shop that compete with the ones that you are trying to sell would be plain stupid. The *Daily Mirror* found itself banned from Bannatyne Fitness premises.

Some customers rebelled. One is quoted by the newspaper as saying 'This ban is disgusting. I'll read my copy in there', and it also quoted Bannatyne's brother Sandy as saying 'To try to ban a national newspaper over a true story is typical of him'.

IT ALL ADDS UP

In less than ten years, Bannatyne Fitness had grown to 61 clubs. Before the takeover it was worth £120 million. Bannatyne identified club sites where he had extra land and came up with the idea of building hotels along side. The club receptions double as check-in for hotel guests and hotel guests can use club facilities. Bannatyne has had offers to buy out the company but he admits that if he did sell, he'd only feel driven to start up something else.

But he also has a whole other career to occupy him with his television shows – the longest running of which is *Dragons' Den*, now in its seventh series. He's written several books, been involved in the launch of a business magazine and is busy acting as a Business Angel to several other entrepreneurs. Over the years he has taken his financial philosophy into other businesses, hacked down expenses claims, cut operating costs, done deals with suppliers, introduced his fixed-rate deals and turned around struggling enterprises. He may have a reputation for being a tough negotiator and a hard-headed, tight operator, but it seems to have stood him in good stead in his business dealings so far.

Bannatyne says his operations haven't been hit by recession. Profits, he says, are up. He's dealt with the financial crisis by capping expansion in the meantime and concentrating on maximizing profits at his existing outlets. Customers who can't afford the luxury of two weeks in the sun can still afford their club membership fees and they might treat themselves to a little extra compensatory luxury while they're there. The recession hasn't been bad for everyone, and Bannatyne's worth is estimated to have risen by about £10 million in the last year.

MAKE MONEY, EXPAND RAPIDLY, THEN MAKE MORE MONEY

- **Bannatyne wants to be the best, not necessarily the cheapest.** Done the right way, adding value to products will mean that you can charge your customers more.
- **Borrow and expand rapidly.** Bannatyne is never afraid of taking on more debt because he's secure in the belief that his businesses will work.
- **Bannatyne negotiates fixed fees for projects** with architects, builders and other professionals, rather than paying by the hour.
- **Look for ways to cut costs at every step along the way.** Bannatyne works out how to maximize income from any project using the minimum number of staff to meet the regulations.
- **Own freeholds rather than renting or leasing**, and always buy new equipment. Integrate facets of the business such as a café and reception areas, so that one lot of staff can cover both areas, as Bannatyne does.
- **Bannatyne utilizes as much space as possible to maximize income.** Forget showy areas such as impressive foyers.
- **Don't spend money you don't need to** and never back someone who doesn't believe in their business enough to risk their own money. Bannatyne believes the best deals are the ones which benefit all parties involved.

9

PUT YOUR NAME OVER THE DOOR

'Every entrepreneur in the world has a big ego – that's why my name is on all my health clubs, all my hotels, everything.'[1]

– Duncan Bannatyne

If you've ever started a business, you'll know how difficult it can be to come up with the right name. The name tells your potential customers something about the business and the products or services you provide. To a certain extent, the name you decide on will depend on what you're selling and who your customers are. If you're a lawyer, you probably wouldn't want to be called 'Lawless and Co.'; if you sell fruit and vegetables, you might want something that suggests you're a greengrocer.

'Duncan's Super Ices' got the message across fairly well. 'Quality Care Homes' wasn't difficult for customers to work out, either. It was chosen because of Bannatyne's commitment to bringing a different kind of care to the UK; quality care in quality buildings. His children's daycare centre chain was named 'Just Learning'. Bannatyne Fitness started out as 'Bannatyne Health and Leisure'. The New Grange hotel in Darlington – his first hotel – became Hotel Bannatyne after a change of business model.

If you've ever started a business, you'll know how difficult it can be to come up with the right name.

To begin with, Duncan's Super Ices was a name that spelled out exactly what was on offer. At that point, the Bannatyne name meant nothing to the ice cream buying public. With Quality Care Homes he made a name for himself in his local area but it wasn't until he set up Bannatyne Health and Leisure that the Bannatyne name started to appear on signs. It is, says Bannatyne, about inspiring him to do his best. Knowing that his name – which has now become a recognizable brand – could be tarnished by poor service and resulting bad publicity is a huge motivator to make sure that all his staff are professional and keep his customers happy.

THE FIRST 'BANNATYNE' VENTURE

As we have seen, the idea of starting up a health club came to Bannatyne when he had a skiing accident in 1993 and he had to use the gym to get his leg working properly again. He just took a few years to bring the idea to fruition.

Quality Care Homes and Just Learning had been taking up all his time and he was constantly looking for new sites for his ever-expanding empire. He was negotiating to buy some land in the middle of a huge housing development near Stockton-on-Tees to build a daycare centre. He bought an acre of land before realizing that he only needed half that. Joanne suggested that he use the other half of the plot to build his first health club on, because it was right in the middle of a big housing development with few facilities.

Bannatyne took his architect to see a health club at Scotch Corner on the A1 and they worked out how to improve on it and make the new club the best in the north-east. Bannatyne still had Quality Care Homes at this stage, but in the end the care homes business was sold well before the paint was dry on the first health club – so Bannatyne was able to focus on building the health clubs into a chain. He and Joanne were running the club from home and were later joined by Tony Bell. Bannatyne had the team, the money and was enjoying himself, but he couldn't work out what to call his new business.

It was Joanne who suggested he use his own name. He was against the idea initially as no one could spell it and he was constantly referred to as 'Ballantyne'. Joanne won the day. 'I had a good personal reputation in the north-east as a provider of quality care: if I put my name to the club, potential members would be more likely to believe it would be a quality club with responsible management.'[2]

The business ethos has to come from the top and be believed in by every member of staff.

It worked and, from the opening, business was brisk. It only remained for Bannatyne Health and Leisure to become Bannatyne Fitness, and he was on his way to becoming a household name. The change came about because Bannatyne thought that in the future he might want to float the company to raise more cash. He checked out the valuations of health and leisure chains that had floated and discovered that the ones with higher valuations had 'fitness' in their names rather than 'health'. Perhaps club users prefer to use clubs with the more positive and aspirational 'fitness' in the title than ones with the slightly more nannyish 'health'. The name has to convey the purpose of your business to the potential customers and 'fitness' seemed a better fit.

BUILDING THE BANNATYNE BRAND

Bannatyne thinks of three words that he wants customers to associate with his business. He wants Bannatyne Fitness to convey 'friendly', 'dynamic' and 'quality'. The ethos is that everything the business does should convey those three words and customers of anything with the Bannatyne name attached should be assured that they will get 'friendly, dynamic and quality'.

Bannatyne believes that to establish the brand you have to give consistency. Customers go back again and again to a company because they know exactly what they will get, and it's something they like, at a price they're willing to pay. Often it's that consistency that keeps them from going elsewhere and trying out what the competition has to offer; they don't want the disappointment of finding they've spent the same amount for something they like less. The brand sets out what customers can expect and delivers their expectations. Any branding specialist will tell you that two identical products or services can be launched at the same time to the same market at the same price, and it's the one that gets the brand right that will take off.

His brand is built around the provision of quality.

For Bannatyne, the company logo, headed paper, website, shop signs should all communicate your values to your customers and so should your staff. If you want to build a successful brand you have to make sure your staff know what the brand stands for and what the values are, and that they are as enthusiastic about it as you are. The business ethos has to come from the top and be believed in by every member of staff.

BE THE BEST

Bannatyne's ethos seems to be about always being the best – the best care homes, the best nurseries, the best health clubs, the best hotels and the best quality properties. It's not about being the cheapest. He works on the principle that people are willing to pay a little bit more to get better quality and that's the market he aims for. For Bannatyne, having his name on his business ventures is there to assure his customers that the club, spa or hotel may not be the cheapest but it is the best.

'Best' is a rather subjective concept. All a business person can do is to look at what the competition is providing and try to improve on it. When Bannatyne Health and Leisure opened its first club in the south of England, they noticed a cultural difference between the members there and those in the north. People in Essex spend a lot more time commuting in and out of London to work and have less time for leisure. Bannatyne discovered that they wanted their children to use the pool while they took an aerobics class. If classes overran, customers got upset. Bannatyne learned to modify each club depending on the lessons they'd learned from the last one and the staff kept a tally of who used the clubs when. From all the information they gathered about their members' habits they tweaked and refined until the club met members' needs as near as possible.

If you give your customers what they expect, plus a little bit more, they'll remain loyal.

Bannatyne has his name over the door and aspires to provide the best of anything he does. His brand is built around the provision of quality. The fitness chain is the business that made Bannatyne seriously rich and made his name; but it was *Dragons' Den* and his media profile that made that name a household one. When he realized that his name had become a 'brand', he knew that he needed to make a few changes. His first hotel, which had been called the New Grange, became Hotel Bannatyne, and he redesigned his logo and used the same one across health clubs, hotels, property developments and all his new ventures. Consistency is the message. It allows customers of any Bannatyne product or service to know what to expect.

THE PERSONAL TOUCH

Since the days when Bannatyne knew the names of the children he sold ice cream to, he has tried to provide a personal service. He has a photo of himself in every club with his contact details so that members can get in touch with him directly if they have any problems. While he claims that he's a natural when it comes to delegation, and not good at the detail, he must be fairly confident that there aren't going to be many problems for him to deal with personally. He believes the best club is always the one that asks its customers about their needs and responds to their answers.

Bannatyne believes in gathering information about your customers that will allow you to understand them better and therefore respond better to their needs. He takes the lessons learned in one venture into the next and subsequent ventures. And he believes that you should look at the areas where your business is doing well, examine why, and then do more of the same in other areas of your work.

REPUTATION AT STAKE

Because 'Bannatyne' is above the door, Duncan Bannatyne's personal reputation is everything. If that reputation were to be called into question because of poor service and failing to meet his customers' expectations, his business could suffer. It's something he seems very aware of. Courting a public profile was therefore a high-risk strategy. He wanted a nationwide profile because he thought it would be good for the business, and the TV shows and the books followed. Had there been skeletons in the Bannatyne cupboard, that's when it would have come out – and if there was damage to be done, that's when it would have been done.

There have been accusations by members of his family that Bannatyne isn't as generous a sibling as he would like to make out. There have been stories of the penny-pinching boss. None of it seems to have done his reputation any harm. That probably indicates that his customers, be it in his clubs or on TV or in print, feel they are relatively unimportant criticisms, and have no impact on the level of service they are getting.

Bannatyne believes in gathering information about your customers that will allow you to understand them better and therefore respond better to their needs.

You only have to think back to the damage done to Gerald Ratner's empire by the joke that one particular item on sale in his shops was 'crap' to see how a damaged personal reputation can affect business. Bannatyne is well aware that if you set yourself up as providing the best, you can't afford to get it wrong.

SO HOW DO YOU KEEP THE CUSTOMERS COMING BACK?

If you give your customers what they expect, plus a little bit more, they'll remain loyal. People prefer what they know and dislike change. Duncan's Super Ices with the funny faces and names delighted the children. Quality Care Homes gave residents facilities they wouldn't get elsewhere. Just Learning gave parents enough local daycare places for their children. Bannatyne Fitness gave people gyms within a ten-minute drive of where they lived. The hotel, spas and property development all pin their reputation on quality and luxury.

When you have a business that has several sites, or you have several businesses, it's hard to keep monitoring to make sure they all live up to your standards. Bannatyne employs mystery shoppers in his health clubs and has regional managers to oversee business in different parts of the country. When he was running several nursing homes, he visited them as often as he could and liked to be there at lunchtime to see what was on the menu. He'd eat with the residents to find out if the food was good enough, the portions big enough and the dishes varied. He is happy to admit that he loved knowing that his homes were making a difference to people's lives but also that he loved knowing he was making himself a fortune.

MONITORING OR SNOOPING?

Rather controversially, Bannatyne has mystery shoppers in his clubs. Staff are told when they're taken on that they could at any time be showing around a mystery shopper posing as a potential customer.

He responds to criticism of that method by saying that if employees don't like it, they needn't take the job offer. He uses the exercises to glean insight into how well his clubs are operating and how morale is among the staff. He also uses it for talent-spotting employees who might benefit from training or qualify for promotion.

SELL THEM MORE

A successful business doesn't just keep its customers; it gets more of their money by offering them new products and services. It's important to respond to the changes in the industry. As the fitness industry introduced new classes and new methods, clubs like Bannatyne's have had to stay in tune or lose customers to newer venues with more modern equipment. You have to be flexible and stay ahead of the competition.

It's much cheaper to keep existing customers and get them to spend more than it is to attract new customers.

Bannatyne keeps one step ahead by asking customers what they want. He doesn't wait for them to complain that he's getting it wrong – he uses a questionnaire or email to ask them periodically what they'd like to be done differently or what new services they'd like, even a suggestions box or a prize for the best suggestions. Bannatyne knows that if customers are getting a great service from you already, they will be more willing to buy another service from you. It's much cheaper to keep existing customers and get them to spend more than it is to attract new customers.

PUT YOUR NAME OVER THE DOOR

- **Be aware of what's at stake.** Putting your name above the door is putting your reputation and your business on the line. Bannatyne knows that he can't afford to get it wrong, especially in 'personal' and 'care' industries.
- **Bannatyne believes his employees have to buy into his values and ideals**, and deliver the best possible service or product to his customers. If they do, those customers will keep coming back and a growing reputation will attract more customers.
- **Sell those customers more.** Like Bannatyne, ask them what they want and give it to them rather than losing them to the competition.
- **Be inspired.** Bannatyne says putting your name above the door inspires you to deliver your promises. Maybe you can't afford not to put your name above the door?

10

GIVE IT ALL AWAY BEFORE YOU DIE

'It's sweet that he likes giving back – but nothing happens in Bannatyne's world unless it happens to him. When he encounters Romanian refugees, he sets up an orphanage. When he visits Ethiopia as a trustee of Comic Relief, he becomes an evangelist for the cause.'[1]

– Ed Caesar, *The Sunday Times*

Duncan Bannatyne became involved in charity work well over a decade ago. He was inspired to become a philanthropist by fellow Scot Sir Tom Hunter, who intends to donate his fortune to good causes within his lifetime. Bannatyne appears to have taken that philosophy to heart too. As they say in his native Glasgow – 'there's nae pockets in a shroud'!

Bannatyne discovered that once you're wealthy, people quickly get to know about it. Being listed in the *Sunday Times Rich List* after Quality Care Homes floated on the Stock Exchange highlighted his wealth in a public way. The steady flow of begging letters started to arrive.

He became involved with the Charter for Business, which funds the Duke of Edinburgh awards scheme that promotes entrepreneurialism in schools. Bannatyne firmly believes in taking the business message into schools and speaks on the subject regularly. On one particular occasion, Gordon Brown was at an event he spoke at and, not long after, the government announced an initiative to teach entrepreneurship.

Duncan Bannatyne became involved in charity work well over a decade ago.

Bannatyne seems to have taken an interest in the requests he received and when an appeal moved him enough, he would help individuals such as the little girl who needed a growth removed from her face. The children of the domestic violence refuge in Hartlepool and their mums had presents from Santa one Christmas courtesy of his team. However, Bannatyne doesn't seem to like handing over money unless he knows exactly how it's going to be used and can see it in action or can visit the end result.

ROMANIA

In 1993 he was contacted by a local policeman who had started a charity to help children in Romanian orphanages. In his self-deprecating style, Bannatyne has recounted how he considered that it might be useful to have a police acquaintance to get him off any parking tickets before he returned the call!

The plight of the orphans came to light when the country's Ceausescu regime was overthrown in 1989. Probably Bannatyne, along with most television viewers in the UK, would have been shocked by the pictures at the time of babies and small children chained to their cots and living in filthy conditions. The policeman, Bob Shields, collected medical supplies in the north-east of England and drove them the 1000 km to Brasov. He needed funds. Bannatyne raised £20,000 with a charity dinner and ball, and that started his long association with Romania.

Bob Shields invited Bannatyne to visit Romania to see what was being done with the money and, in 1995, he went. What he saw in terms of human suffering astounded Bannatyne. The institute in Brasov that Bob took him to had 96 patients, four toilets and one bath. It was one of the better places, as the funds they'd collected had made a difference.

Bannatyne also saw the problems Bob was up against in doing anything to help. Within 24 hours a lot of the drugs, clothes and mattresses they'd taken with them, donated by people in the UK, had gone missing. Some of the people working in the institute were so badly paid they sold the donated stuff to feed their own children.

After that first visit, one of the Quality Care Home nurses went to Romania each time medicine was sent and stayed for a few weeks to teach the staff and care for the patients. Applying his business mind to the situation, Bannatyne also hired his own company pharmacist. This meant that they could send unused medicines from his care home patients to Romania. There was an added advantage in that by having his own pharmacist, the company could pay trade prices for some of their everyday supplies and make cost savings. As Bannatyne says in connection with so many of the solutions he comes up with to business challenges – it's better if there's a benefit to all parties involved. Even a charity can benefit from having a business perspective applied to it.

Even charities can benefit from having a business perspective applied to it.

UNICEF

When Bannatyne saw a 1997 TV appeal for Unicef, the United Nations organization that cares for children around the world, he responded with a cheque. A few weeks later he was invited to a dinner to hear Lord Deedes talk about his work with Unicef and realized that he wanted a real connection with the projects he funded. He was keen to give more money but he wanted to see where that money went and how it was used. And in particular he wanted it to be used in Romania.

Unicef started to fund small homes where children had much better care. By then Bannatyne had decided that he wanted to fund projects that had a long-term benefit, and educational projects seemed to best fit his criteria. On one visit he was taken to a housing estate where his money had been used to fund several children's education. He was horrified to discover a filthy hovel but astounded to see the children come down the stairs in immaculate school uniforms paid for by his money.

A CONTINUING COMMITMENT

Since his first trip to Romania the country has changed dramatically, but Bannatyne says there's still work to be done. He has taken journalists there and shown them the side of the country that no one wants to talk about any more – the children still living in sewers and rubbish dumps. He also persuaded his good friend John Moreton to become involved; together, they funded the building of homes for Roma Gypsies.

Bannatyne still goes to Romania regularly. One of the people he met through his charity work and who he credits with having given his life an added dimension is Magnus MacFarlane-Barrow, who runs a charity called Scottish International Relief. They went to Romania together in 2002 to see the house MacFarlane-Barrow had bought and renovated to house homeless children. He wanted to build another in the same grounds so all the children could stay together. Bannatyne gave him the money he needed, as long as he had the house ready for Christmas. It was a tight deadline but one that Magnus accepted and managed to meet. The house was named Casa Bannatyne.

In July 2009 Bannatyne returned to Romania at the invitation of Adela, one of the first orphans to be housed in Casa Bannatyne.

She was getting married and as Bannatyne told Sharon Hendry of *The Sun* he was delighted to be asked to give her away. Bannatyne does appear to be genuinely something of a 'big softie', especially where children are concerned.

Bannatyne asks members of his health clubs to make a voluntary donation of 25 pence a month

Bannatyne asks members of his health clubs to make a voluntary donation of 25 pence a month on top of their membership fees to fund projects like Casa Bannatyne. The scheme raises tens of thousands of pounds a year, which is enough to pay salaries and teach and train workers, and so helps Romania to build its own future.

OTHER PROJECTS

Bannatyne has also become involved with projects around the world through Magnus MacFarlane-Barrow and Scottish International Relief. He has paid for an orphanage to be built for street children in Colombia and is involved with Mary's Meals in Malawi. It's another food and education project where children are given lunch if they go to school. This encourages them to go, so they get food and an education, and, because they are fed, they concentrate better. Mary's Meals provides the food if local community people cook it and 100,000 children are fed by the project.

In 2006 Bannatyne became involved with a group of UK-based millionaires called Entrepreneurs Unite. They took a trip to South Africa in conjunction with Richard Branson's Virgin Unite and heard pitches from budding entrepreneurs there. It operates in a similar

THE CROWNING GLORY

In 2004 Bannatyne got a letter telling him that 'the Prime Minister is minded to recommend you to the Queen to receive an OBE for services to business and charity …'.

way to *Dragons' Den*, but any profits go back into the company to create more jobs.

He's also involved in a UK network of entrepreneurs whose aim is to get together with the business leaders of the future and give them a helping hand. In 2008 he set up his Bannatyne Charitable Fund and put £1 million into it. Bannatyne is also President of No Smoking Day, a trustee of Comic Relief and was voted Most Admired Celebrity Charity Champion by *Third Sector* magazine in November 2008. He was named an Honorary Fellow of Unicef in 2003 and appointed a Unicef UK Ambassador in February 2009.

Bannatyne had decided that he wanted to fund projects that had a long-term benefit.

He recently told an interviewer from *The Guardian* that 'it's absolutely not a guilt trip and it's absolutely not "giving back", because I've never taken anything. I can help, so I help, and that's it.'[2]

The value of education and the capacity of coming generations to build their own future never seems to be far from Bannatyne's mind when he gets involved in charities. He is mainly involved in children's charities and many have an educational element. Perhaps it's a throwback to his own childhood, and the desire never to be poor, that drives him to help other children around the world and give them the wherewithal to step out of poverty for good.

But, ever the canny businessman, Bannatyne never loses an opportunity to point out that his giving is done in the most tax-efficient way. When he gave Magnus MacFarlane-Barrow money to build the children's home Casa Bannatyne in Romania, he knew that it would be subject to tax relief from the government! Even when he's giving with one hand, he's doing the calculations with the other.

He is always business-orientated in everything he does, even in charity.

He is always business-orientated in everything he does, even in charity. He also expects the same results from people working in charity as he does in business. MacFarlane-Barrow was set a deadline for opening Casa Bannatyne when the money was handed over and met it. The home was opened in time for Christmas. Bannatyne seems almost in awe of the results MacFarlane-Barrow achieved by applying business methods to charity budgets.

THE FUTURE

And so what will happen to that estimated £320 million he's worth when he dies? Will his six children get to live in the lap of luxury for the rest of their lives without having to lift a nicely manicured finger?

Not a bit of it. Bannatyne revealed in *Anyone Can Do It* that when he sold Quality Care Homes, he set aside £3 million for their trust funds: he feels they would lack the drive and ambition to make the best of themselves if he left them his entire fortune. Even the money in the trust fund comes with strings attached; Bannatyne's a man who likes to be in control. His children won't get the money if they smoke. His hatred of smoking is well documented. He made a programme for the BBC in July 2008 where he gave the tobacco industry a typical Bannatyne drubbing. He denies he's being controlling and says his children can smoke if they like; they just won't get their inheritance.

It seems that 95% of Bannatyne's fortune may go to charity.

GIVE IT AWAY BEFORE YOU DIE

- **It's more than just a donation.** Bannatyne prefers to have a real connection with the charity projects he funds. That way, he can see what his money is being used for and be sure that it's making a difference.
- **Support causes you're close to.** Bannatyne supports many children's charities. He seems to have a genuine love for children and his projects are about helping them to improve their lives and prospects. Much of the money he donates goes to food and education projects in countries like Malawi. Education is the thing Bannatyne feels is most likely to help children out of poverty.
- **Bannatyne likes to see business principles applied to the charity work he supports.** People like Magnus MacFarlane-Barrow get Bannatyne's approval because they can manage to do more on their small budgets than many entrepreneurs can with vastly bigger sums. He also believes in making his donations in the most tax-efficient way possible.
- **Pass the message on.** As well as charities, Bannatyne believes in supporting schemes that will help enterprising young people become successful entrepreneurs and taking that message into schools.
- **Share the wealth?** Bannatyne believes in helping charities because he can and has pledged to give much of his fortune away. His own family will be expected to make the best of their own chances rather than living off their inheritance.

DUNCAN BANNATYNE AND BBC'S *DRAGONS' DEN*

'His put-downs have caused him to be dubbed the Simon Cowell of the Den, and he is often assailed by members of the public seeking to pitch their entrepreneurial ideas.'[1]

– David Cohen, *Evening Standard*

Bannatyne has told interviewers that he wanted a national profile because it would be good for business. Was it profile that Bannatyne wanted – or fame? There's a thin line between the two. Perhaps 'profile for the sake of the business' sounds more acceptable than fame for its own sake. Bannatyne has achieved both and while profile may have helped him be heard by the great and the good, it must surely be fame that brought him an invitation to Elton John's birthday party. And they've both helped him make money.

BANNATYNE THE SHOWMAN

Dragons' Den wasn't the first time Duncan Bannatyne ventured onto the public stage. It may be the show that made him a household name and gave him the profile he wanted, but he'd started down the showbiz route many years earlier.

His first foray into the world of entertainment was when he was still at school. Bored and on the lookout for something more exciting, he found a book in the library on magic tricks. He taught himself how to do a few and used them to mesmerize his friends. A few shows for the Boys' Brigade followed and he relished the attention.

In his 50s his TV career was prefaced by an attempt to get his name in lights on a bigger screen. It was 2002. The businesses were going well, with Bannatyne Fitness well established. Nigel Armstrong and Tony Bell were effectively running the show. His divorce was behind him and he was living with Joanne and their two children. It seems that boredom had set in again and he was looking for something else.

THE ACTOR'S LIFE FOR ME!

Then something else turned out to be drama in the true sense of the word. He and Joanne were at a charity auction where one of the lots was a walk-on part in Guy Ritchie's film *Revolver*. He bought the lot and joked that Ritchie might recognize his talent and offer him a bigger part. Alas, that didn't happen – but the seed was sown. Bannatyne wanted a new career in acting. Joanne may have thought he'd taken leave of his senses, but she soon realized he was serious about giving it a go.

She enrolled Duncan in a month-long intensive drama course at the New York Academy of Acting … in London. Joanne and he weren't married at the time and decided to end their relationship, but they remained good friends and parents to Tom and Emily. Bannatyne set off to London to seek fame and profile.

Bannatyne has told interviewers that he wanted a national profile because would be good for business.

He enjoyed drama school so much that he enrolled in a summer school at the Royal Academy of Dramatic Art (RADA) in London with people from all over the world. He bought a flat in the city and a house around the corner from Joanne in the north-east. While he was at acting school, his TV career began to take off too. *Mind of a Millionaire* exposed him to his classmates as the wealthy entrepreneur he'd avoided telling them he was.

Eventually, Bannatyne's list of acting credits extended to parts in a few student films and a few paid roles, including ones in the Kelly Brook film *School for Seduction* and in a pilot for a soap called *Girls' Club*, playing the accused in an episode of *55 Degrees North* on the

BBC, and his biggest role as a gangster who drowns in an episode of the BBC drama *Sea of Souls*.

So his acting career might have taken off, but by the time the *Sea of Souls* episode was broadcast he was already a Dragon and likely to be recognized as such. And he was finding that there aren't many parts written for men his age!

BECOMING A DRAGON

Dragons' Den has been Bannatyne's biggest hit. He's taken part in *Mind Your Own Business*, a daytime makeover programme, and *Mind of a Millionaire*, in which psychologists analyze entrepreneurs to see if they act differently to employees. But with seven series of *Dragons' Den* under his belt, he's a household name. At last he has the profile he wanted. As he explained in an interview in May 2008, his fame is different from that of, say, a TV presenter: 'Myself and the other Dragons don't call it fame, we call it profile. It's profile for the businesses that we have created.'[2] He's found fame in the most appropriate way: hand in hand with business.

With seven series of *Dragons' Den* under his belt, he's a household name.

The 'Den' format came from Japan and is used around the world. Everywhere people are the same, enterprising, aspiring entrepreneurs who passionately believe in their business ideas and who need funding and expertise to help them get established. The five Dragons all have different skills, attributes and areas of expertise. They've made their fortunes in different sectors and have their own investment criteria. They're interested in different businesses and bring different perspectives to the analysis of each idea they're presented with.

Bannatyne is straight-talking and forthright. What comes across is that for him, the person is the important thing. If he doesn't like you, feels you've been economical with the truth or doesn't feel you're passionate and committed, it doesn't matter how good your idea is – he's out. Interesting, given he also claims not to be a good people manager. He wants to know that you're putting your own money into the business too. That way, he knows you really believe in it and will fight for it. If entrepreneurs aren't prepared to take a loan on their homes or want the Dragons' money to pay themselves a salary, Bannatyne is likely to question their belief and commitment.

He's found fame in the most appropriate way: hand in hand with business.

The Dragons also have several things in common. They're all successful, are investing their own money and are on the look out for viable opportunities. They want to make money. Bannatyne already had a record of putting his own money and expertise into other people's businesses and helping to turn them into successes. He'd invested in Alpha Radio and New Life Care Services, and turned them around. But he'd also invested in the Lady in Leisure gyms and had to walk away, he ultimately lost more than £1 million.

THE SHOW'S THE THING

Despite not being in *Dragons' Den* for the fee, which isn't big, the ever-prudent Bannatyne got his agent to put a clause in the programme contract that would ensure that no other Dragon got paid more than he does. After that – and with some voice coaching, to make his accent easier to understand – Bannatyne was ready for anything the programme threw at him.

At the time of writing, he's invested more than any of the other Dragons, with £1 million of his own money going into 17 ventures featured in the programme. What he's looking for is a return of around 20–25% a year on his investment. Evan Davis, the show's presenter, says Bannatyne is a surprisingly conservative investor, playing relatively safe. Viewers could be forgiven for wondering why, given his personal history and unconventional business approach, he's unsympathetic to people with little experience and dismissive of high-risk ideas. Now that he's the investor, he can be as cautious as some of the bank managers he was refused money by in the past.

Some people assumed the Dragons would just put up the money and let them get on with running their businesses, but there aren't many entrepreneurs who'd be willing to do that. Investors invest because they want to make a return on their money, which usually means keeping an eye on the way the business is run. Bannatyne also wants to know when he's going to get his money out. Entrepreneurs want to take their money and invest in something new, and most want their money out in three years. Bannatyne will be flexible and tie money up for longer if he likes the company. He also looks for businesses he can add value to and will learn something from, and that will be fun. But essentially he likes to help businesses grow, sell and move on.

Bannatyne has turned down the opportunity to invest in several projects that proved to be winners. When asked how he could make such mistakes, he defends his decisions by saying that if anything he said to a would-be entrepreneur during the programme helped them to build a better business then that was a success rather than a failure. Not all investors want to invest in the same ventures and where one investor helps make it a success, it might have done less well with another because of different areas of expertise. The same is true in real life; there aren't mistakes just different decisions.

SPOTTING POTENTIAL

Since first appearing in 2005, Bannatyne has agreed investments in the Den that total £1,150,000 in 17 businesses. Apart from Charles Ejogo and Elizabeth Galton (who he initially invested money in but later withdrew from), some of the others are:

- **Alistair Turner and Anthony Coates-Smith, Igloo Thermo-Logistics:** Temperature-controlled transport for transporting perishables around the UK. He invested with Richard Farleigh.
- **Paul Tinton, Prowaste Management Services:** This deals with construction waste and recycling. He invested in this with Deborah Meaden.
- **Denise Hutton, Razzamataz:** Bannatyne had invested in stage schools (Stage Coach) before and did well when he sold his shares, so he invested in this chain of dance, drama and singing schools. 'It was a no-brainer, which is why for the first time on *Dragons' Den* history I made the investment without negotiating the equity. She was selling the company too cheap and it was crazy that the others didn't see it.'[3]
- **Tony and Steven, UK Commercial Cleaning:** Bannatyne has said the main reason he invested in this industrial cleaning company was the men.

- **Sharon Wright, MagnaMole:** This was an invention to thread cables through cavities in walls that looks like being the most successful ever *Dragons' Den* pitch. Bannatyne invested in this with James Caan (with whom he also invested in the remaining pitches on this list).
- **Andrew Harsley, Rapstrap:** A reusable plastic strap similar to cable ties, but the excess can be reused.
- **Peter Moule, Chocbox:** A patented plastic box enclosing electrical connections. Bannatyne and Caan are building up a portfolio of related technical products.
- **Janice Dalton, Blinds in a Box:** Temporary window blinds.

DRAGONS AT WAR

Bannatyne claims to get on well with his fellow Dragons – past and present – but there are undoubtedly tensions between him and Peter Jones. Jones made his feelings clear after he and Bannatyne agreed to invest in Charles Ejogo's Umbrolly umbrellas, which were to be sold from vending machines in London's Underground network.

Bannatyne initially managed to invest the same amount of money as Jones, but for 2% more of the equity in the company. It's just not done in the Den for one entrepreneur to take a larger equity share for the same amount of money as another. Jones was peeved! Bannatyne claimed it just showed what a shrewd, tough operator he was. They resolved the issue by calling Charles back to the Den and giving him back the extra 2% equity, but Bannatyne never admitted he was in the wrong.

Bannatyne and Jones can still be seen to have the odd onscreen snipe at each other. It makes great viewing. On the BBC documentary on Duncan Bannatyne, Peter Jones admitted that in the first series he had little time for him, but says he discovered Bannatyne's a good evaluator of people and is a big softie deep down. Theo Paphitis said in the same documentary that the pair are 'like lovers: they can't live with each other and can't live without each other'. In Bannatyne's video diary for the 2009 series, the pair were seen larking around very amicably – so how much of the 'tension' is for public consumption?

So far he's invested more than any of the other Dragons.

Bannatyne's most used and best beloved words in the Den are 'ridiculous', 'ludicrous' and 'I'm out!' One of the words often used about Bannatyne by the presenter is 'canny' – not so much mean and tight as prudent and thrifty.

Naturally, along with Barber, we probably all prefer to see the nasty one because it makes better TV – but Bannatyne claims it's all down to the way the programmes are edited!

Bannatyne may be reluctant to admit making mistakes on the show but he does admit to learning a lot from it, such as learning about patent law because it wasn't an area he was familiar with. He also feels he learns a lot from the other Dragons because they all look at business propositions differently and respond differently to pitches. He feels that no matter how long you're in business, or how successful you are, there are so many ways to run a business that you never stop learning.

THE WORST PITCH

Despite the fact that it was in the first series in 2005, Bannatyne still remembers one particular pitch. It seems to have made a lasting impact and gets mentioned regularly in interviews.

Gayle Blanchflower had spent £60,000 on the worldwide rights to cardboard beach furniture. She intended it to carry advertising and promotions. Bannatyne asked what would happen if it rained. 'She looked at me with what appeared to be pure hatred in her eyes. "You don't go to the beach if it rains, stupid." I didn't much like being called stupid. So what happens if my little boy Tom comes out of the sea and sits on a chair? "Well tell him not to. Discipline your children."'[4]

Bannatyne and the rest of the Dragons were 'out'. Gayle was presented with the best environmental product award at the 2007 British Female Inventors and Innovators awards ceremony, but according to records at Companies House the business has since been dissolved.

THE BOTTOM LINE

When Bannatyne invests in someone he comes across in *Dragons' Den*, it looks as if all the haggling is done with the offer. But it isn't simply a case of 'I'll give you £100,000 for a 20% stake in your business'; Bannatyne, like the other Dragons, has his own investing criteria.

He only appears to invest in people he likes and trusts. If he thinks you're lying to him, he'll bow out. If you're asking for too much money for too small a stake and he can't see how he can make at least a 25% return, you're likely to be on a loser. And woe betide the entrepreneur who doesn't want to risk their own money in their own business. Why would a Dragon take the risk when the business owner won't?

However, the TV programme is only the start of the process. After a successful pitch, the due diligence process starts. That's the legal process or research that goes through everything about the company with a fine-tooth comb before the Dragon's money goes into the business. Bannatyne and his fellow Dragons will want to know that everything the business person has told them is true, that orders are real, that the patent is valid, the structure of the company is as they expected and that contracts are contracts. That's what happens in the real world when Angels invest. It can take up to six months. It would be a very naïve entrepreneur who invested in another company without due diligence.

There are so many ways to run a business that you never stop learning.

Often the offers made and accepted in the Den don't materialize once the due diligence process has been completed. Peter Jones and Duncan Bannatyne jointly agreed to invest in Umbrolly and businessman Charles Ejogo. He had a contract with London Underground to put vending machines with his umbrellas in their stations. On the show Charles had told the Dragons he wouldn't have to pay for this, but on scrutinizing the contract they discovered he would have to pay £2000 per machine per year and when he had more than 50 machines he'd have to pay a one-off £1 million. Peter Jones tried and failed to negotiate a better deal and so the investment fell through.

Similarly, an offer to jewellery designer Elizabeth Galton in the first series came to nothing: 'I thought she was a high-risk investment, but the chance of owning a percentage of a future designer label offered a very big reward.' Bannatyne and fellow Dragon Rachel Elnaugh invested, but the relationship with Rachel ran into trouble and she withdrew. Bannatyne put up £10,000 to keep Elizabeth going while they renegotiated his investment, but while that was going on Elizabeth had another offer of investment from someone who saw the original show repeated. A week later, Bannatyne got a cheque for £12,500 – a £2,500 profit – and that ended his association with the jeweller.

For most Angel investors, the lure is a good return on their money and the chance to carry on in business after they've sold off their own businesses, or while their own businesses are doing well without much of their input. Most will also want a say in how the business is run. After all, it's their money. For many business people that's the advantage and the disadvantage. Some appreciate the chance of having access to the expertise that the Angel brings; others see it as interference in how they run their business.

Most investors also want to know not just how much money they'll get back on their investment, but when they'll get their money back. While Bannatyne is fairly flexible, he'll want to have an exit strategy in mind. The aim could be for the business person to buy him out, for Bannatyne to sell his share of the business or for the company to be floated on the stock market. He'll also want to know what his money will be used for. If it's to be used for starting production, increasing output or a marketing push, he's likely to be happy. But he's unlikely to be impressed if the business person says it will be used to allow him or her to leave their job and give them a salary.

SEEKING INVESTMENT FROM DUNCAN BANNATYNE

Outside the Den, Bannatyne has dozens of requests from budding entrepreneurs for investment – mostly by email, but occasionally someone stops him in the street. If you do, you risk the Dragon's wrath – remember how he reacts on the TV programme. If you try to lie or can't answer his questions (especially ones about your costs and projected profits), and you don't tell him exactly what he'll get out of it and when – forget it. He's likely to be 'out'.

BANNATYNE THE AUTHOR

Not only is Duncan Bannatyne's face well-known from *Dragons' Den* and the other TV shows he's appeared on, it's a fairly common sight on the business and biography shelves in bookshops and on the internet. To date, there's *Anyone Can Do It: My Story* (Orion, 2007), *Wake Up and Change Your Life* (Orion, 2009), his guide to setting up and making a success of your business venture, and *How to be Smart with Your Money* (Orion, 2009), a guide to making your money work for you.

You'd be forgiven for thinking that the Bannatyne you see on TV and interviewed in the press is a different Bannatyne from the one of the books fame. He claims to be a businessman who operates on gut instinct, who isn't a people manager, who thinks networking is for wimps and never gives his business plan a second glance – but *Wake Up and Change Your Life* reads like many of the traditional business guides. He claims delegation is the key to the success of his empire, so true to form; he delegated the writing of his books to a ghost writer.

Bannatyne does a lot of public speaking on running a business and various business topics, including the anti-smoking legislation in the workplace. He also gets requests to appear on all sorts of other radio and TV shows as a guest. And he became involved with setting up a magazine about entrepreneurialism called *The Sharp Edge* after being interviewed by a journalist who was looking for a business partner.

With that kind of press and media profile and all the businesses he's invested in on *Dragons' Den*, it's no wonder Bannatyne doesn't have time to be in the office more than five hours a week these days and leaves the running of his own businesses to Nigel Armstrong and Tony Bell. But what he's doing is part of the business too – it's all part of building the Bannatyne brand and raising that profile. It's all part of the marketing and a means to attract customers.

Another spin-off of his fame was being asked to try show jumping for Sport Relief's TV series *Only Fools on Horses*. Twelve celebrities were to be trained to show jump, the public would vote for them to stay or go, and money would be raised along the way for tackling poverty and helping disadvantaged people in the UK and around the world. Bannatyne enjoyed the training but got unseated at a crucial moment and was out before the filming started, nursing a fractured radius. Theo Paphitis and Peter Jones, his fellow Dragons, who had each pledged £12,500 if Bannatyne won, were able to return their wallets to their pockets.

THE POWER OF PROFILE

> *'Television has given me a voice in government that I didn't have and would never have got without it.'*[5]

These days, even Gordon Brown knows who Duncan Bannatyne is. After one particular speech on teaching entrepreneurship in schools, the government announced a new initiative on just that. Whether that was inspired by what he had to say Bannatyne doesn't know, but he feels that he was listened to on anti-smoking legislation and that without *Dragons' Den* that wouldn't have happened. For that reason, he'd like to keep his role in the 'Den'.

His high profile has spawned all sorts of public reaction too. The Facebook group 'I hate Duncan Bannatyne' has been replaced by 'Duncan Bannatyne has the most Asymmetrical Face I've Ever Seen'. On a more positive note, there's also 'I'd Let Duncan Bannatyne into My Den' and 'I want to be Duncan Bannatyne'.

IS PROFILE GOOD FOR BUSINESS?

At the beginning of the first series of *Dragons' Den*, Bannatyne's personal fortune was estimated as more than £130 million. As the seven series have been aired, those estimates have risen steadily – by series six, he was said to be worth £310 million and despite the recession, that's gone up to £320 million.

It's difficult to quantify the impact of the public profile, but he claims that *Dragons' Den* has pushed sales of his books into the millions. And he is convinced that without his TV profile, he would never have been taken seriously as a bidder for the 24 health clubs he bought from the Hilton Group in 2006, and that he's more likely to get the big loans he needs to expand his empire. Bannatyne attests to being interested in profile but not fame – but whichever way you look at it, it seems to be getting the desired results.

RECESSION? WHAT RECESSION?

At the time of writing, all seems to be rosy for the UK's favourite serial entrepreneur. Perhaps it's partly because he's not so much serial as diverse. He has a whole raft of businesses of varying sizes and has invested in many more. He may not make a lot from his TV shows, but they've certainly given him the kind of profile that boosts book sales. He may not have a lot of ready cash, but his personal business holdings are estimated to be worth £320 million.

Canny as ever, Bannatyne's approach to the economic downturn is to put expansion on hold and concentrate on maximizing profits. While many business owners have had to make do with breaking even and forget about making a profit, accounts filed at Companies House show Bannatyne Fitness in rude health. It made a pretax profit of £8.2 million, which compares very favourably with the £2.7 million profit for 2007. In a recent interview with bmmagazine.co.uk, Bannatyne explained that he had made the conscious decision to focus on integrating the 24 Living Well clubs he'd bought from the Hilton Group in 2006 into Bannatyne Fitness and improving its operations.

It seems to have been the right decision. Membership of gyms and health clubs is holding well. People may cut down on expensive treats in times of economic uncertainty but if they've paid a gym membership, they're more likely to use it and once they're in the health centre they may spend a bit more. Bannatyne told the magazine that his members are becoming more profitable, with the average yield per club member is up from £32.63 to £33.31 last year.

In another recession-defying move, Bannatyne announced the opening of a new city spa in Edinburgh earlier this year. He says its aim is to take advantage of the British people's decision to pamper themselves in the UK rather than go abroad for expensive holidays.

The company has been keeping the bank happy by meeting the interest payments on its loans from cash flow, so it looks to be in a very healthy position. Later in the aforementioned interview, Bannatyne said that 'we are finding it not very challenging. We're 2% up on last year. We are finding it hard to believe ourselves.'

THE LAST WORD

Duncan Bannatyne has made his millions through hard work, commitment, an eye for the main chance, an ability to put a new spin on an existing idea, and hiring the right people.

While he makes it all look easy, he does his research and planning, understands the importance of being in the right place at the right time, and knows his own strengths and weaknesses, building his businesses around his strengths and hiring people to fill the gaps left by his weaknesses. Above all, he believes in hiring the right people and delegating to them as much as possible while he gets on with growing the business and looking for the next opportunity. He has also learned to take the lessons from each project with him into the next, refining and improving as he builds his empire.

He sees himself as a maverick but is he really unorthodox, a dissenter with no time for rules and regulations? While he is undoubtedly independent and single-minded, he's rather more conventional than he'd like us to believe. What makes him a bit different is that he's had to learn the hard way without the help of the traditional textbook or the hand-holding benign mentor. He's a self-made millionaire with a villa in France, but few of the other affectations that go with it.

For now, Bannatyne shows no signs of slowing down. As he assured the *Darlington and Stockton Times* in November 2006: 'I'll never, ever retire because I enjoy it all so much … Besides, retirement means giving up.'[1] It was a promise he reiterated after his 60th birthday party in 2009, when he told David Roberts of the *Northern Echo* that 'retirement is not even in my vocabulary and anyway, as far as I am concerned, 60 is the new 40.'[2]

His passion for business keeps driving him but perhaps his need to be in control is a contributing factor. What is certain is that he's probably telling the truth when he says – as he did in his video diary for the last series of *Dragons' Den* – that it's not about the money. He's made much more than he could ever need or could ever have hoped for. He claims that he spends just five hours a week in the office, but that's the man's artifice. He certainly does more than five hours a week in total when you take into account public appearances, *Dragons' Den* and his charity work, and who knows how many working hours are spent on the phone or email, by the pool, keeping an eye on things back at the ranch. This is a man who will always be looking for the next deal, the next money making venture. The old entrepreneurial restlessness seems unabated.

Whether you love him or hate him, you can't take it away from Bannatyne that he's a success. He has wealth, fame, profile and as many of the trappings as he desires. He's been there, got the T-shirt and written the books on how to do it. But there lies the paradox: anyone with the entrepreneurial attributes that Bannatyne admires wouldn't need the books – they would be out there giving it a go themselves.

NOTES

THE LIFE AND TIMES OF DUNCAN BANNATYNE

1 BBC, online video of Duncan Bannatyne, *bbc.co.uk/dragons-den/dragons/duncanbannatyne.shtml*, undated.

2 Barber, Lynn, 'The interview: Duncan Bannatyne', *The Observer*, 18 February 2007.

CHAPTER ONE

1 Pool, Hannah, 'Question time: Duncan Bannatyne', *The Guardian*, 4 June 2009.

2 Bannatyne, Duncan, *Wake Up and Change Your Life*, Orion Books, 2008, p. 15.

CHAPTER TWO

1 Card, Jon, 'Duncan Bannatyne', *growingbusiness.co.uk*, 23 May 2008.

2 Bannatyne, Duncan, *Wake Up and Change Your Life*, Orion Books, 2008, p. 80.

CHAPTER THREE

1 Bannatyne, Duncan, 'Simplicity always succeeds, just look at *Dragons' Den* and MagnaMole' *The Daily Telegraph*, 30 July 2009.

CHAPTER FOUR

1 Bannatyne, Duncan, *Wake Up and Change Your Life*, Orion Books, 2008, p. 59.

CHAPTER FIVE

1 Bannatyne, Duncan, *Wake Up and Change Your Life*, Orion Books, 2008, p. 124.

CHAPTER SIX

1 Anonymous, 'Driven, restless and a bit arrogant – but definitely not the retiring kind', *Darlington and Stockton Times*, 4 November 2006.
2 Bannatyne, Duncan, *Anyone Can Do It: My Story*, Orion Books, 2006, p. 158.

CHAPTER SEVEN

1 Burn-Callander, Rebecca, 'Duncan Bannatyne – Bannatyne Fitness chain', *realbusiness.co.uk*, 1 July 2009.
2 Bannatyne, Duncan, *Wake Up and Change Your Life*, Orion Books, 2008, p. 108.

CHAPTER EIGHT

1 Dalgrano, Paul, 'In the *Dragons' Den* with God', *Sunday Herald*, 6 September 2008.

CHAPTER NINE

1 Burn-Callander, Rebecca, 'Duncan Bannatyne – Bannatyne Fitness chain', *realbusiness.co.uk*, 1 July 2009.
2 Bannatyne, Duncan, *Anyone Can Do It: My Story*, Orion Books, 2006, p. 205.

CHAPTER TEN

1 Caesar, Ed, 'Duncan Bannatyne: he breathes fire on his own family', *The Sunday Times*, 15 February 2009.
2 Pool, Hannah, 'Question Time: Duncan Bannatyne', *The Guardian*, 4 June 2009.

DUNCAN BANNATYNE AND *DRAGONS' DEN*

1 Cohen, David, 'Duncan Bannatyne: I'd love to show Madonna what we have built in Romania', *Evening Standard*, 3 July 2009.
2 Card, Jon, 'Duncan Bannatyne', growingbusiness.co.uk, 23 May 2008.
3 BBC, *Dragons' Den: Success, from Pitch to Profit*, HarperCollins, 2008, p. 180.
4 Bannatyne, Duncan, *Anyone Can Do It: My Story*, Orion Books, 2006, p. 261.
5 Barber, Lynn, 'The interview: Duncan Bannatyne', *The Observer*, 18 February 2007.

THE LAST WORD

1 Anonymous, 'Driven, restless and a bit arrogant – but definitely not the retiring kind', *Darlington and Stockton Times*, 4 November 2006.
2 Roberts, David. 'Bannatyne tells birthday guests: I will never retire', *The Northern Echo*, 9 February 2009.'

READING LIST

BOOKS

Bannatyne, Duncan, *Anyone Can Do It: My Story*, Orion Books, 2006, p. 261.

Bannatyne, Duncan, *Wake Up and Change Your Life*, Orion Books, 2008, p. 108.

BBC, *Dragons' Den: Success from Pitch to Profit*, HarperCollins, 2007, p. 180.

ARTICLES

Anonymous (1), 'Driven, restless and a bit arrogant – but definitely not the retiring kind', *Darlington and Stockton Times*, 4 November 2006.

Anonymous (2), '*Dragons' Den* star Duncan Bannatyne tells *Mirror*: you try being boss', *Daily Mirror*, 21 January 2009.

Anonymous (3), 'Fitness chain in top health', *Evening Gazette* [Middlesbrough], 22 May 2009.

Anonymous (4), 'Dunc SOS', *The Sun*, 25 June 2009.

Anonymous (5), 'Duncan's backing', *Evening Gazette* [Middlesbrough], 6 August 2009.

Armstrong, Kathryn, 'A Dragon at ease', *The Journal* [Newcastle upon Tyne], 13 June 2009.

Bannatyne, Duncan, 'Simplicity always succeeds, just look at *Dragons' Den* and MagnaMole' *The Daily Telegraph*, 30 July 2009.

Bannatyne, Duncan, 'Business is about more than just the bottom line', *The Daily Telegraph*, 5 August 2009.

Barber, Lynn, 'The interview: Duncan Bannatyne', *The Observer*, 18 February 2007.

Bath, Richard, 'No business like show business', *Scotland on Sunday*, 22 February 2009.

Blackley, Michael, 'Dragon defies gloom with city spa launch', *Evening News* [Edinburgh], 17 June 2009.

Brown, Annie, 'Dragon's ten: Scots tycoon Duncan Bannatyne's top tips for beating credit crunch', *Daily Record*, 19 May 2009.

Burn-Callander, Rebecca, 'Duncan Bannatyne – Bannatyne Fitness chain', realbusiness.co.uk, 1 July 2009.

Caesar, Ed, 'Duncan Bannatyne: he breathes fire on his own family', *The Sunday Times*, 15 February 2009.

Card, Jon, 'Duncan Bannatyne', growingbusiness.co.uk, 23 May 2008.

Carroll, Sue, 'Dunc's a drag for daughter', *Daily Mirror*, 27 January 2009.

Cohen, David, 'Duncan Bannatyne: I'd love to show Madonna what we have built in Romania', *Evening Standard*, 3 July 2009.

Collins, David and Gregory, Andrew, 'The I Hate Duncan Bannatyne Society? I'm in says his brother', *Daily Mirror*, 27 January 2009.

Dalgrano, Paul, 'In the *Dragons' Den* with God', *Sunday Herald*, 6 September 2008.

Hazeldine, Simon and Gregory, Joe, *Bare Knuckle Negotiating*, Lean Marketing Press, 2006.

Knight, Kathryn, 'Slaying of a Dragon', *Daily Mail*, 2 February 2009.

McGrath, Nick, 'Under the microscope: Duncan Bannatyne', *Daily Mail*, 10 March 2009.

McLauchlan, Karen, 'Degree for a Dragon', *Evening Gazette* [Middlesbrough], 11 February 2009.

Moyes, Stephen and Armstrong, Jeremy, 'Dragon's dumb', *Daily Mirror*, 21 January 2009.

Moyes, Stephen and Collins, David, 'TV Dragon charges for freebie bar', *Daily Mirror*, 17 January 2009.

Pool, Hannah, 'Question time: Duncan Bannatyne', *The Guardian*, 4 June 2009.

Quade, Gemma, 'Crunch time! The Dragons are back – and defying the recession', *The Sun*, 11 July 2009.

Robinson, Karen, 'Here be Dragons', *The Sunday Times*, 28 June 2009.

Sale, Jonathan, 'Passed/failed: an education in the life of Duncan Bannatyne, entrepreneur and *Dragons' Den* panellist', *The Independent*, 19 March 2009.

Scott, Caroline, 'The soft-centred Dragon', *The Sunday Times*, 21 June 2009.

Stewart, Stephen, 'Dragon Duncan: I sell my rubbish on eBay', *Daily Record* [Glasgow], 25 May 2009.

WEBSITES

bannatyne.co.uk
bbc.co.uk/dragonsden
bbc.co.uk/dragonsden/dragons/duncanbannatyne.shtml

INDEX

A WHOLE SHELF OF BUSINE$$ BIG SHOTS

Let us teach you everything *they* know

14855 02/10

LIZ BARCLAY

Liz Barclay is a freelance broadcaster, writer, communications trainer and business coach. She has presented various programmes on BBC Radio 4 for the past 11 years including the daily consumer programme *You and Yours* and the review programme *Pick of the Week*. She writes on business and personal finance for newspapers and magazines including the *Independent on Sunday*; has produced and presented 60 small business programmes for BBC 2; runs the website moneyagonyaunt.com and plans to launch a new site for SMEs in the spring of 2010. She has written several books including *Small Business Employment Law for Dummies* and is an experienced conference speaker and facilitator.